P9-CRQ-727

Growing
Your Church
Through
Training
and Motivation

Library of Leadership Development
Marshall Shelley, General Editor

Leading Your Church Through Conflict and Reconciliation
Renewing Your Church Through Vision and Planning
Building Your Church Through Counsel and Care
Growing Your Church Through Training and Motivation

9708

LIBRARY OF Leadership DEVELOPMENT

Growing Your Church Through Training and Motivation

30 Strategies to Transform Your Ministry

Marshall Shelley, General Editor

BETHANY HOUSE PUBLISHERS
MINNEAPOLIS, MINNESOTA 55438

Published by Bethany House Publishers
A Ministry of Bethany Fellowship, Inc.
11300 Hampshire Avenue South
Minneapolis, Minnesota 55438

Printed in the United States of America.

Library of Congress Cataloging-in-Publication Data

Growing your church through trainig and motivation : 30 strategies to transform your ministry / by Marshall Shelley, general editor.
    p. cm. — (Library of leadership development)
   ISBN 1–55661–967–7
   1. Christian leadership. 2. Church growth. 3. Pastoral theology.
   I. Shelley, Marshall. II. Series.
BV652.1.G76 1997
   253—dc21   97–33840
                                                  CIP

Contents

93996

Part 4
Board

Part 5
Individual

Part 6
Congregational

Introduction

Great tectonic plates in the church and culture
have slid sideways.

—Kevin A. Miller

While you and I have been quietly serving in ministry, the ground on which we stand has shifted. Great tectonic plates in the church and culture have slid sideways, collided, pushed up new mountain ranges, caused quakes. In religion in America, "The past three or four decades have brought radical changes," writes church consultant Lyle Schaller.

Among those radical changes, many deal directly with the theme of this book—training and motivation. In fact, they call for this volume.

In Schaller's words:

- There are a growing number of churches "organized around the central goal of *challenging the laity to be engaged in ministry* while the paid staff 'runs the church.' "
- There has been a "change in emphasis in congregational strategies from converting nonbelievers to *transforming believers into disciples.*"
- There is also now "a societal-wide demand for excellence, including high-quality preaching, teaching, meeting places, children's ministries, and *training experiences for lay volunteers.*"

One result of all these changes, Schaller concludes, "is a plea for relevant help."

How can you motivate people to care, to get involved, to pray, to lead? How can you help them find just the right spot for service? Keep them motivated? Boost their flagging morale?

We have prepared this book with one goal: to provide you with relevant help for questions like these. Tested wisdom. Godly counsel. Proven strategies.

To do that, we assembled twenty-nine veteran church leaders who know how to do training and motivation—and who can teach others how to do it. You'll learn from Rick Warren, Marlene Wilson, John Maxwell, and more than a score of others. They teach not only the basics but the advanced, behind-the-scenes knowledge that's worth so much.

I pray that as you read, *you* will be trained and motivated and that you'll pass that on to the people who are looking to you.

—Kevin Miller
Editor
LEADERSHIP

Contributors

Leith Anderson is pastor of Wooddale Church in Eden Prairie, Minnesota, a suburb of Minneapolis. A contributing editor of LEADERSHIP, he is author of *Dying for Change* and *A Church for the Twenty-First Century*. He is also coauthor of *Mastering Church Management, Who's in Charge?* and the tape series *The Best Is Yet to Come*.

Daniel Brown is founding pastor of The Coastlands Church in Aptos, California. He has written *Unlock the Power of Family*.

John Cheydleur is a Salvation Army officer and psychologist who currently serves as a program-development officer for forty-one adult rehabilitation centers in ten eastern states. He is author of *How to Find and Be Yourself* and *Every Sober Day Is a Miracle*.

Don Cousins is founder and director of T.D.I. (Team Development, Inc.), a nonprofit organization that assists church leadership teams in carrying out their ministry. Before that he was associate pastor at Willow Creek Community Church in South Barrington, Illinois. He is coauthor of *Walking With God, Networking* and *Mastering Church Management*.

Gary Fenton is pastor of Dawson Memorial Baptist Church in Birmingham, Alabama. He is coauthor of *Mastering Church Finances*.

Carl F. George is a church consultant. He is author of *Leading and Managing the Local Church, Breaking Growth Barriers*, and *The Coming Church Revolution*.

Richard C. Halverson (1916–1995) was former Senate chaplain and longtime pastor of Fourth Presbyterian Church near Washington, D.C. He was a member of LEADERSHIP's inaugural advisory board.

Jack Hayford is pastor of Church on the Way in Van Nuys, California. He is author of many books, among them *Worship His Majesty* and *Rebuilding the Real You*, and coauthor of *Mastering Worship* and *Who's in Charge?*

Roberta Hestenes is pastor of Solana Beach Presbyterian Church in Solana Beach, California. Before that she was president of Eastern College. She is author of *Turning Committees Into Communities* and coauthor of *Mastering the Art of Teaching*.

Ken Horton is pastor of McKinney Memorial Baptist Church in Fort Worth, Texas.

David Hubbard (1928–1996) was president of Fuller Theological Seminary for thirty years. He was general editor of *World Biblical Commentary Series* and author of four commentaries: *Proverbs, Joel, Amos*, and *Hosea*.

Joel C. Hunter is pastor of Northland Community Church in Longwood, Florida. He is author of *The Journey to Spiritual Maturity, The Challenging Road*, and *Prayer, Politics, and Power*.

Bill Hybels is founding pastor of Willow Creek Community Church in South Barrington, Illinois. He is author of, among others, *Descending Into Greatness* and *Rediscovering Church*, and coauthor of *Mastering Contemporary Preaching* and *Fit to Be Tied*.

Wayne Jacobsen is director of Lifestream Ministries in Visalia, California, a ministry to encourage spiritual intimacy and Christian community. A contributing editor of LEADERSHIP, he has written *The Naked Church, Tales of the Vine*, and *In My Father's Vineyard*.

George Mallone (1944–1995) was pastor of Grace Vineyard Christian Fellowship. He authored *Arming for Spiritual*

Warfare, Those Controversial Gifts, and *Furnace of Renewal.*

John Maxwell is founder and president of INJOY, an international leadership development institute. Before that he served as pastor of Skyline Wesleyan Church in San Diego, California, for fourteen years. He has written, among others, *Developing the Leader Within You* and *Developing the Leaders Around You.*

Bob Moeller is a contributing editor of LEADERSHIP and radio host of *The Marriage Minute.* He has written *For Better, For Worse, For Keeps* and *The Stirring.*

Robert J. Morgan is pastor of Donelson Fellowship in Nashville, Tennessee. He is author of *Empowered Parenting* and *On This Day: 365 Days With Preachers,* and editor of *The Children's Daily Devotional Bible.*

Ron Oertli is a regional director of the church discipleship division of the Navigators. He is author of *Right Fit.*

Charles M. Olsen is director of Worshipful Work, a center for transforming religious leadership. He also serves as interim executive director and program director of Heartland Presbyterian Center in Parkville, Missouri, outside of Kansas City. He is author of *Transforming Church Boards Into Communities of Spiritual Leadership* and *The Base Church,* and coauthor of *Discerning God's Will Together.*

Larry Osborne is pastor of North Coast Church in Vista, California, a suburb of San Diego. He is author of *The Unity Factor* and coauthor of *Measuring Up.*

Ben Patterson is dean of the chapel at Hope College in Holland, Michigan. Before that he pastored Presbyterian congregations in New Jersey and California. He is a contributing editor to *Christianity Today* and LEADERSHIP, author of *Waiting: Finding Hope When God Seems Silent,* and coauthor of *Mastering the Pastoral Role* and *Who's in Charge?*

Roy C. Price is pastor at Monte Vista Chapel in Turlock, California.

Ruth Senter is on the faculty of Trinity Evangelical Divinity

School. She is author of numerous books, including *Have We Really Come a Long Way?*, *Longing for Love: Conversations With a Compassionate Heavenly Father*, and *Beyond Safe Places.*

Al Sibello is production manager and editor of Practitioners Publishing Company in Fort Worth, Texas.

Fred Smith, Sr. is a business executive living in Dallas, Texas. He is a recipient of the Lawrence Appley Award of the American Management Association. He is a contributing editor to LEADERSHIP and recently retired from the board of directors of Christianity Today, Inc. He has written *You and Your Network* and *Learning to Lead.*

Roger Thompson is pastor at Berean Baptist Church in Burnsville, Minnesota.

Rick Warren is founding pastor of Saddleback Community Church in Orange County, California. He is author of *The Purpose-Driven Church*, *Answers to Life's Difficult Questions*, and *The Power to Change Your Life.*

Marlene Wilson has served as faculty director for twenty-five years of the volunteer management program for the University of Colorado in Boulder. She is author of *The Effective Management of Volunteer Programs*, *How to Mobilize Church Volunteers*, and *You Can Make a Difference.*

Part 1

Mission

1

The Potential Around You

*I'm always asking, "How can I add
value to the person I lead?"*

—John Maxwell

Investing in people is like investing in stocks. High risk can
bring a huge return or a huge loss. The greatest leaders will
help you the most—but they can also hurt you the most.

The best leader on my staff once took a hundred of our people and started a new church a few blocks away. The way he
did it crushed me. Another staff member was accused of a moral
failure. He told me he was innocent, and I defended him. I
found out three months later that he had, in fact, committed sexual sin.

These weren't leaders left from some previous administration. I had identified their potential and poured my life into
them. For months I told myself, *I'm never going to let staff get
close to me again. They'll never hurt me or lie to me again.*

Then one day I realized, *John, this is the dumbest thing
you've ever done.* When we embrace people and pour our lives
into them, they'll sometimes hurt us. But the future of our ministry and our churches depends on developing others to lead.

My eyes were opened to this truth in my first church. When
I went to Hilliham, Indiana, I could count the people on one
hand. Over several years, I worked night and day, and the
church grew to over three hundred. I really thought I had done

something, not realizing that my self-reliance would break me.

When I left that church, attendance dropped from three hundred to less than one hundred in only a few months. I realized I had failed. I had not prepared others to lead. I vowed, *This will never happen again.* Since then, one of the primary focuses of my ministry has been leadership development.

One thing this emphasis has taught me is that developing leaders is hard. People willing to be developed are pretty scarce. When you do find them, they're usually already over-committed in other arenas of life.

On top of that, it's tough to build a team with leaders. You can't herd cats, and you can't herd leaders. They are strong-willed and usually have their own agendas.

Then, as if all this weren't enough, strong leaders are hard to keep. They will be continually enticed with other opportunities that appear to be more exciting and meaningful.

So how do we invest our lives in others in a way that brings great dividends for the kingdom of God?

Value Added

My development of leaders begins with a clear purpose. I'm always asking, "How can I add value to the person I lead?" I advise pastors not to go to a new church and ask, "Who's going to help me?" Instead, look around, find out who the leaders are, and ask, "How can I add value to them?"

We can do this in several ways.

One is to ask people to be part of a great vision. Having a cause worth dying for is the greatest reason to live. This is enhanced when you treat people as your greatest asset. We all believe this is true when we first meet people, but after we've worked with them awhile and seen their weaknesses, it's a little tougher to believe.

Adding value also comes from listening to people. If I know their heart, I know exactly where to add value. I develop the part of them they want to see developed, not what I happen to need at the time. This prevents me from using people.

Or I ask, "What is their unique contribution?" Then I equip people according to their gifts and desires.

For example, our new marketing manager for INJOY is a young man named Kevin. Kevin brings some excellent skills from the business world. For the next several months, he'll be traveling with me and getting to know my heart while I get to know his. I'm putting all the leadership material I can find in front of him, and he's digesting it as quickly as I can provide it. I'm feeding a hunger that is already there.

And then, of course, I simply coach people. When Dan Reiland was a member at Skyline, he felt called to ministry and went to seminary. During this time he came back for a year of internship on our staff. Dan is smart and highly task-oriented, but also melancholic and nonrelational.

His first week on the job he walked right past me and seven or eight other people in the lobby. He never said hello or acknowledged our presence. With his briefcase in hand, face forward, he headed for his office, work on his mind. I thought, *He didn't even see us.*

So I followed him into his office and said, "Dan, you just passed by your work."

"What do you mean?"

"We were standing in the lobby, and you walked right by without speaking."

"Man, I'd like to talk, but I've got work to do."

"These people *are* our work, Dan," I said. "We're in the people business."

What I love about Dan is that when he saw his need for change, he did something about it. I began to teach people skills to him. After five years, he became my executive pastor and did nothing but people development and oversight. He came with me to INJOY, and he told me the other day that 140 people are coming to his house for Memorial Day. He has become the Pied Piper.

The Art of Unique Development

Of course, part of the art of leadership development is being sensitive to the need to work with individuals in unique ways.

Some people have a heart for God but no leadership skills. With them we need to provide on-the-job training. If people have the character qualifications, they merely need to learn how to maximize their efforts.

As we seek to develop such people, either we or they can worry too much about position and titles. I teach them, "Wherever you're working, whatever organization you serve, start adding value to people and begin to gain their respect. They will champion you." When they understand that leadership is influence instead of position, everything changes. They don't have to strive to be leaders; if they strive to add value to others, others will allow them to be leaders.

Other people have great influence but little spiritual depth.

Sometimes that's our fault. As a gifted business leader once told me: "Monday through Saturday I'm challenged to the limit. I'm taking risks; I'm making deep commitments in my business. But when I go to church, I'm never challenged or asked to make deep commitments. I'm never asked to take a risk."

This grieves me. Most churches have some wonderful leaders who are only nominally spiritual because they've never been challenged, when, in fact, it's easier to bring people around spiritually than it is to raise them up to a place of leadership.

But leaders who lack spirituality must be developed on the side. They can't be put immediately into leadership in the church without compromising the spiritual integrity of the congregation. Rather, I would pour my life into such a leader by praying with him, teaching him to pray Scripture, getting him involved in some accountability group.

Great leaders make good advisers. I've approached businesspeople and said, "You're good at finances. Would you advise me?" As we relate, they get a heart for the things I have a heart for. Then, as they begin to show spiritual leadership, I put them over some project with a specific deadline—maybe looking for land for the church or planning a men's retreat. Then I watch how they interact.

Some leaders blossom through involvement on boards and committees, while others can't operate within the confines of that kind of structure. It's simply not their world.

Recognizing Potential

I compare leadership development to an elevator ride, with the destination being the tenth floor. Sometimes, when we get to the third floor, the leaders we're developing say, "This is my floor, I'm getting off."

My tendency in the earlier years was to get off with them. "Let's take some stairs. We don't need to get on the elevator. Let's go just a little bit higher."

My wife, Margaret, finally said, "John, you have to let others determine what level they want to live on." That wasn't easy for me because I think growth is life.

Over the years my philosophy of leadership development has been forced to change. I used to think I could lead anybody, but I found out there are some people I can't lead. In addition, I used to think anybody could be a leader if he was really committed. That is naïve. There are a lot of people who don't want to be leaders, nor are they cut out for the job.

Knowing these realities, how do we choose the right people to develop for leadership?

First, I think we should give our present leaders our best shot. There are many people I was ready to write off after the first month who later became tremendous assets to the work.

I urge pastors to give themselves six months to assess their current leadership's potential for personal growth. You play the hand you've been dealt. You'll find some people have a lot of potential, while others have little. You pour yourself into the first group, then you figure out where the others might fit in to other areas of ministry.

In my first church, one man was highly critical of me. I went to him and said, "I'm sorry if I've done something wrong." I thought we'd embrace and everything would be fine. I hugged him, but he didn't hug me back. I didn't confront him or initiate any kind of change, and the next week he was after me again. He was not the kind of person I needed on my leadership team.

When I approach a potential leader, I ask him to become my prayer partner for at least a year. That gives us time to get to know each other's heart.

On the front end of these relationships, I ask, "Are you willing to reproduce other leaders if I invest in you?" This perpetuates the culture of leadership development and weeds out people who probably wouldn't have developed anyway.

Sometimes intimidation keeps pastors and high-octane lay-leaders from connecting with each other. The pastor looks at the leader and thinks, *He's got a company and a big budget. I have this little church and a part-time secretary.* But the business person looks at the pastor's world and thinks, *He's been to seminary. He knows Greek and Hebrew. I could never achieve that level of spirituality, that godly focus.* So intimidation goes both ways.

Personal Leadership

Often the obstacles to developing leaders are not within others but within ourselves.

A key personal issue we must settle before we can develop others is whether we are ready to give up power. The only people who can empower others are people who can easily relinquish power.

I can do that when I realize there is an unlimited supply available to me. If this is the only paper clip I think I'm ever going to have, I'm not going to give it to you; I need it. But if I know we've got 10,000 paper clips in the supply closet, I'm going to say, "Want a paper clip? Have a whole box."

So I'd suggest pulling together the gifted leaders in your church and letting them recruit and develop potential leaders. That requires tremendous security within the pastor, but we'll have that security when we understand what fosters loyalty from the congregation's leaders. Loyalty is the result of respect. You won't be loyal to a person you don't respect. In my dad's day, the pastor got loyalty because he was the pastor. These days, people will not be loyal to anyone unless they respect the person and know the leader respects them. People give loyalty when they can say, "I'm a better person because of that leader."

Even the pastor who doesn't feel like a strong leader can develop others to be leaders if he is secure not only in turning over leadership to others but also in showing a willingness to develop himself. Any pastor who recognizes the importance of leadership will develop his or her own skills.

A second personal issue that enables us to be more effective in developing leaders is learning to be *passionate* about ministry rather than *driven*. There was a time when I was driven. I was too impatient, too goal-oriented. Today, though, I would say I'm a passionate leader. I think there's a world of difference between being driven and being passionate when it comes to leadership. One who is driven tries to prove something to someone, to seek approval for something. He focuses on the goal alone. One who is passionate in leadership savors the journey as much as the destination. The one who is driven usually depends on the attention of others; the passionate one works from a spiritual center within. Driven people burn out. Passionate people do not.

A third personal issue is whether or not I am willing to admit my limitations. Knowing my limitations brings me greater spiritual health and enables me to foster the same openness in the leaders I am training.

For example, I am only now getting a better perspective on the inevitable fatigue of ministry. I used to think fatigue was the price you paid for working for God. But I no longer believe that the most spiritual people build the biggest churches or work the hardest. Fatigue is no indication of spiritual maturity. My motivation for admitting and dealing with fatigue comes from knowing how vulnerable it makes me to sin and error.

What's Your Passion?

Not long after I came to Skyline, I was leading a conference in Jackson, Mississippi, when a guy said, "We wish you'd give us ongoing leadership training."

I responded, "Well, if I did a tape each month on leadership, how many of you would join the club?"

Thirty-seven people raised their hands. I wrote down their names and said, "Okay, I'll go home and teach my staff. We'll put it on tape. I'll send it to you."

That's how the INJOY Life Club started. Dick Peterson, an IBM executive and member of our church, said, "I've got a heart for pastors. I'll help." He put a tape duplicator in his garage and a computer in his bedroom, and this thing just exploded.

About five years ago, one of my trustees sat down and said, "John, you're going to have to make a choice."

I said, "No I won't. I love both the church and INJOY. I've got to do both."

He said, "We support you, but we believe there's going to be a time when you will have to choose."

Four years later, I finished a conference in Cincinnati, where over a thousand kids came forward to answer the call to full-time ministry. I sat down at the end of that service and thought, *This is life. This is what I was born to do.*

Going back to my hotel that night, I finally admitted to myself, *I can no longer do both.*

When I got home, I walked into the house and said to Margaret, "I can't do both."

She responded, "Do you realize that in the twenty-five years we've been married I've never heard you say, 'I can't do this'?"

I began to cry. "But, Margaret, I *can't* do this. I have too much on me. I'm not good enough, fast enough, big enough, or smart enough." For the rest of my life, I'll be focused on multiplying leaders.

Everywhere I've served, I've prayed for God to send me leaders to build his church. For fourteen years, at least once every month or so, I'd meet someone visiting Skyline for the first time. We'd introduce ourselves. Then God would speak to me and say, *John, here's one.* It was the most humbling thing to me because I didn't do one thing to bring these people in.

After I resigned, I was together with about seventy-five church leaders at a farewell dinner. I got up and said, "All my life I've prayed for leaders. Let me tell you how God answered those prayers."

Then I went around the room telling each one about the time I met them and how God had said, *Here's one.* By the time I was finished, we were all bawling.

Someone asked, "How could you remember meeting everyone in a church this size?"

I replied, "I don't remember meeting every person. But I remember meeting those people I prayed God would lead into my life and whom he indicated to me as potential leaders."

If you pray for leaders, if you have a heart to develop, lead, and empower people, and if you've got a God-given vision, God will give you your heart's desires.

2

Working Through Leaders

*The seeming drawback of too little time to train others
is actually more of a mental block than
a true drawback.*

—Don Cousins

G rowth inevitably leads to chaos.
I don't mean the kind of chaos caused by weak administration or poor planning. I mean the turmoil that accompanies action, the disruption that results from change, and the problems that surface from incorporating new workers into a ministry. An organization without this kind of chaos probably isn't making much of a mark. I'll take chaos—with impact—any time over a calm lack of fruitfulness.

While chaos may not be a comfortable state, the inconveniences it brings are a small price to pay for the thrill of knowing one's ministry is making a difference. And when great things are happening in a ministry, people tend to step forward and ask, "How can I help?" They *want* to be part of the activity—even somewhat chaotic activity—when they see the fruit it bears.

The man who runs our small-group ministry owned a real estate company before he joined our staff. A year or so before he came on staff, he said to me, "I can tell my passion is changing. I used to want to pour all my time into the marketplace. Now I've tasted what it is to be used by God, and I want to invest myself more fully in things that really matter."

People like this, who arise from congregations as volunteers or paid staff, can lighten the load that active ministry creates. They can be channels through which we accomplish the work of the ministry. The only catch is that they have to be properly managed.

Overcoming the Drawbacks

The pastor overloaded with demands may cringe at the prospect of recruiting and supervising other workers. If he has insufficient time to do immediate tasks, how will he ever find time to enlist others in ministry?

Unfortunately, some leaders believe their primary responsibility is to keep the ministry running smoothly, to check chaos at any cost. So they devote the bulk of their time to the immediate tasks that keep their ministry under control. They maintain the ministry. They put out fires. But they never take the steps that would move their ministry forward.

This maintenance mindset has to be reversed. Short-term focus must make way for long-term perspective. We need to ask, "What decisions or activities will help me to be more effective a year from now than I am today?" The answer to that question will determine what we should do first.

Once again, it's a question of A and B priorities. B priorities maintain the ministry, and chances are they scream the loudest for our attention. But A priorities move our ministries forward. So we need to spend the best hours of our day on A priorities, even if that means setting aside a beckoning pile of B priorities.

After fifteen years in ministry, I have concluded that recruiting and training leaders should always be near the top of a manager's A priorities. If we want our ministries to grow, we must nurture people who can take over a portion of our work and expand it. The time required to do this often seems like a drawback, but it gives us back the time in the end.

Take hospital visitation, for example. On any given day, it

would be easier for a pastor to make a hospital visit alone than to recruit volunteers, take them with him, and teach them to make hospital calls. If he went by himself, he could gain time—that day. But the following year he'd still be in the same position: personally making all the hospital calls. And each call would take him away from other necessary activities.

But let's say that early in the year he invested A-priority time in recruiting and training people gifted and called by God to be hospital callers—people with potential to do it more effectively than he. By year's end, they could cover the ministry of hospital visitation and free him to pursue other A priorities. His initial investment of time would quickly save him hours each week and also enable others to use their gifts in meaningful ministry.

Many church leaders bear incredible loads because they haven't mastered the art of raising up fellow leaders and releasing responsibility to them. So they work sixty to seventy hours a week (or more) and produce less fruit than a leader who works reasonable hours but has learned to tap the potential of others.

At Willow Creek, we want our staff to be around for the long haul. We also want them and their families to enjoy life and one another; we don't want to provoke spouses to anger or cause children to grow up resenting the church for taking Mom or Dad away. So we encourage staff to limit their ministry responsibilities to an average of fifty hours a week, and that includes their participation in church services and small groups.

We also know a staff member won't draw others into the kingdom or into leadership unless he exhibits joy, and joy springs from a refreshed life. Who would want to take on the mantle of ministry responsibility if it looks like one big pain?

What keeps ministry from becoming an overwhelming burden? A healthy, shared leadership role. I asked one of our singles ministry directors who came to us from a plush position in business, "Do you ever miss the marketplace? You had more freedom and less pressure, and you certainly made more money."

"No way!" he replied. "I wouldn't go back for a minute. Sure, the ministry is demanding. But I have a great team of workers who help meet the demands. With the fruit my family and I are harvesting and the sense of God's pleasure in what we're doing, there's no way I'd go back now."

Would he feel the same if he hadn't shared his ministry with others? Not on your life. The hours would be killing him, and he'd want out. Fortunately, he took the time early in his ministry to train helpers, and now he's reaping the reward of a manageable ministry. As he learned, the seeming drawback of too little time to train others is actually more of a mental block than a true drawback.

Of course, not all drawbacks are mental blocks. For example, sometimes I make mistakes in choosing people to become leaders. I invest myself in people who don't pan out or never reach the levels I expected. That's frustrating, but a reality.

Every leader must be willing to make mistakes, because we all will. One year I had to let go three staff members who were close friends of mine. All three were men of character who loved the Lord and fit our staff relationally, but their ministries had passed them by. They had ministered effectively to 150 people, but they couldn't handle 200 or 250. Their ministries were suffering, and they were under tremendous pressure.

Decisions like that are tough to make and even harder to carry out. But if we seek and obey God's direction, we can trust him to bring about a resolution in time. For a while my relationships with these former staff members were strained because my decisions had complicated their lives. Today, however, they all are pleased with their career or ministry opportunities, and together we can thank God for his wise guidance.

Most leaders begin ministry fully intending to work through others to demonstrate the priesthood of all believers. But some have drifted away from that principle after getting burned. They selected a wrong person, and the choice came back to haunt them. If that happens three or four times early in one's ministry, the natural tendency is to decide never again to touch the hot stove.

That's unfortunate, because occasional failures don't mean the principle is defective; the practice merely needs refining. When fear arises, it's time to look back and determine where the breakdown occurred: *Did my selection process fall short? Did I fail to train people properly?*

It helps to remember that Jesus was deserted by all twelve of his disciples in his hour of greatest need. If Jesus experienced that kind of fallout, who am I to think I can avoid it totally? I shouldn't quit pursuing sound practices just because of occasionally poor performance.

Other drawbacks of working through others center on the personality of the leader. Personal insecurity may make one think, *If I raise up others to do part of my work, will I lose my uniqueness, my status? And what if they use their new abilities to undercut me?* Those with an unhealthy need to be in control will hesitate to let others into the circle of responsibility.

Good leaders, on the other hand, keep their eyes on the big picture and say, "Building the kingdom of God and seeing this person develop his or her potential—even if it's greater than mine—is more important than protecting my territory."

In reality, accomplishing the work of the ministry through others usually makes the leader look better than ever. More work gets done. More ministry takes place. And the leader becomes respected as a recruiter, trainer, and delegator.

I use a circle to represent what a person can accomplish, given his or her capacities, gifts, energy, and availability. Obviously, any one person's circle is limited; it cannot expand without the addition of another person's resources. Thus, the scope of a ministry remains limited when only one person works in it.

We try to teach our staff to invest their lives in people who have the potential to do one of two things: *expand* the staff member's circle of ministry, or *replace* him or her in the circle. After two or three years of training, the one being trained ought to contribute enough to free the staff member to expand the ministry or to hand it over and move on to a new endeavor.

That has been my experience at Willow Creek. I started the high school ministry, founded our singles ministry, and then developed our small-group ministry. At each juncture, I stepped out of one responsibility and into another, primarily because someone was ready to assume my place. By grooming others to take over my responsibilities, I've freed myself to broaden the scope of our church's ministry. Had I not done so, my contribution never would have expanded beyond my initial circle of ministry in the high school department.

A leader, by implication, is a person who draws others into effective ministry. The key to doing this is to select potential associates with care.

What to Look for in Leaders

In seeking leaders, the temptation is to look first for an individual with tremendous gifts and abilities. At Willow Creek we've learned, however, that this is not the place to start.

Character

The number-one leadership criterion is strength of character. This cannot be compromised. Spiritual intensity or raw ability may appear more important, but we've learned the hard way that they are not.

By his mid-twenties, a person's character is relatively set. If someone is hard-working, honest, conscientious, and loyal in his twenties, he'll probably still be that way in his forties or sixties. Likewise, if there's a major flaw, it probably won't change without extensive work more akin to reparenting than discipleship.

A twenty-five-year-old who doesn't tell the truth likely has worked on the art of deception since childhood; it's doubtful he'll change after one conversation about dishonesty. The same holds true with a lack of personal organization or discipline. To change that requires a major reweaving of the fabric of the person's character.

No matter how gifted, trained, or spiritually mature a person is, the true usefulness of those attributes will be determined by character.

How does one assess character? The two indicators I watch are how people manage their personal life and how they relate to others.

A prerequisite to leading others is the ability to lead one's own life effectively. That's what Paul meant in 1 Corinthians 9:27: "I beat my body and make it my slave so that after I have preached to others, I myself will not be disqualified for the prize." A leader's first responsibility is to have his or her life in order.

Weak character will manifest itself in a lack of self-management: poor self-discipline, tardiness with appointments, incomplete work, being controlled by outside circumstances, or even moral lapses.

Years ago we hired a staff member whose gifts and spiritual intensity appeared unquestionable. We learned after hiring him, however, that he tended to twist the truth. On numerous occasions staff members discovered he had told them conflicting stories. He eventually began pitting one staff person against another, and relationships began to break down.

He also exaggerated. We'd ask, "How many were at that meeting last night?"

"Oh, hundreds," he'd say.

When we knew differently, we'd confront him: "Was it really hundreds?"

"Well, maybe 150." Even after several conversations like this, he continued to exaggerate, and we realized his repeated exaggerations were another form of deception. We all make mistakes, but a continuing pattern such as his indicates a character flaw. Because he failed to recognize it and do something about it, we had to let him go.

Often manifestations of character weakness aren't readily

apparent. That's why it's so important to observe prospective
leaders over time.

The second indicator of character is interpersonal skills.
Some people can relate only in a hierarchy: up and down a
chain of authority. They can work *for* people and/or *over* people, but they can't work *with* people. If the essence of leadership is to get close enough to people to equip them for ministry,
a key ingredient for success is the ability to work *with* people.

Interpersonal skills involve humility, courtesy, patience,
self-control. Someone who exhibits these qualities likely has a
healthy character and is eligible for leadership responsibility.
Conversely, if a person can't relate warmly to others, I question
his or her readiness to lead. I don't have time to build basic interpersonal skills into those I'm training for leadership.

Self-esteem, while not strictly a matter of character, comes
sharply into play at this point. To a degree, all of us have a frag-
ile self-esteem; all of us, because of sin, remain somewhat insecure. While that kind of universal insecurity need *not* hinder
ministry, more pronounced insecurity definitely has a destructive effect. As I mentioned earlier, an insecure person is unable
to rally strong people for fear one of them may be stronger than
himself and thus a threat.

When we interview potential staff and key layleaders, we try
to determine how they perceive themselves. Can they say, "Yes,
I'm a sinner. I'm thoroughly aware that apart from the grace of
God I am nothing, but with the grace of God and the gifts he's
given me, I have something to offer"? The healthier the self-
esteem, the better the foundation upon which to build ministry.
If we compromise here, we'll pay in the end.

Spiritual authenticity

The second criterion for potential leaders is spiritual authenticity. Have they made a mature, consistent commitment to
Christ? Does the Word of God impact their daily lives? Do they
pray? Are they in submission to the Holy Spirit?

I ask specific questions to detect this quality: "What have

you studied in your quiet times this week? Can you share some recent answers to prayer? What are the temptations you struggle with most? How did you come to know Christ? Have you been discipled? Have you discipled someone else?" These questions get at the heart of a person's walk with God more than a general "How's your spiritual life?"

Why is it necessary to discuss such basic spiritual issues? Because people who carry the weight of leadership need to practice the fundamentals. A football player who says "I don't need to practice all week. I can go out on Sunday and play the game" is headed for trouble. Eventually his lack of preparation will catch up with him. It's the same with Christian leaders. To effectively *promote* spirituality one must *practice* spirituality.

Ministry fit

Often people speak of ministry fit strictly in terms of gifts and abilities, but these aspects are only part of the match. Equally important is *passion*. People can be perfectly gifted for a particular ministry, but if they don't have a corresponding passion for it, they'll lose motivation and eventually quit.

We look for potential leaders who say, "God has given me a burden to work with high school students. I've just got to figure out a way to do it." Sometimes that passion isn't evident initially, and we have to draw it out. But even then we need to see a natural spark.

Spiritual passion is an unquenchable desire to *do* something for God. It may not manifest itself in intense emotion, but it always manifests itself in action. The passion may be as dramatic as William Booth's desire to minister to the poor, or as unassuming as a treasurer's desire to protect a church's financial integrity. In either case, God has so created and motivated a person that he or she says, "I feel strongly about this, and I have what it takes to meet the need. Let me at it!"

At Willow Creek, we have people who get emotionally charged about doing building maintenance. They want to present the unchurched with a clean, inviting building on Sunday morning. They also believe the condition of our building should reflect our commitment to an excellent, perfect God. So they're excited about what they do. That's ministry fit.

Relational fit

Leaders who want a well-functioning team also need to choose members who fit relationally. Christian leaders sometimes skip this point because it smacks of favoritism. Aren't we supposed to love everybody? Aren't we called to be tolerant? How, then, can we say a potential colleague might not fit relationally? For the furtherance of the kingdom, shouldn't the leader be willing to swallow his own preferences?

Yes and no. Does a leader need to be flexible? Yes. Should the leader bend to the point of selecting colleagues he or she doesn't enjoy being with? I don't think so. Work usually suffers when there's an uncomfortable team relationship.

Certainly we're to love everybody, but that doesn't mean we have to work closely with everybody. Why did I marry my wife instead of some other girl? One reason was that our chemistry was right. During the course of dating, I realized I liked her more than the others; we got along better; our lives meshed.

Why do I work better with some staff members? Because we happen to "click." Even if we didn't work together, we'd enjoy spending time together. Why not enhance my enthusiasm and productivity by bringing on people with whom I fit relationally?

Every work team has a unique personality. One aspect of Willow Creek's staff personality, for example, is a willingness to flex for the sake of the ministry, to share ideas, and to learn from others. Therefore, if a superstar arrives saying, "I know what I'm doing. I can handle things—my way!" he or she is going to bump heads with other staff members here. But a worker who is teachable—whether a rookie with raw abilities or an experienced veteran with honed talents—will enjoy a natural relational fit.

Traits to Reconsider

While certain personality traits mark leadership candidates as obvious front-runners, other traits may surprise us. In particular, we need to look carefully at aggressiveness and initiative.

Some people equate leadership with personal aggressiveness, but in reality leaders come with a variety of styles and temperaments. Some may be quiet and lead primarily through their actions. For example, former Chicago Bears linebacker and captain Mike Singletary didn't say a lot, but his character and discipline made him a respected leader both on and off the field.

Other effective leaders are naturally shy and avoid the spotlight at all costs. The men who head our sound and lighting ministry don't enjoy getting up in front of people and aren't particularly social, but that doesn't hinder their ministry. They relate well to workers who also enjoy behind-the-scenes work. Their more introverted personalities are precisely what make them effective production leaders.

The key to yet other leaders' effectiveness is their sincerity. They're not aggressive; they don't push hard. But their depth of feeling and passion grips the people they lead.

Pure aggressiveness, rather than suiting a person for leadership, should actually signal caution. Often, an extreme degree of aggressiveness indicates a character problem. The aggressiveness may flow from repressed anger or an inordinate desire to be successful. Such aggressiveness doesn't fuel ministry; it blows it up.

What fuels ministry is initiative. An initiator takes action, but unlike the purely aggressive person, he does it for others' sake rather than his own.

To distinguish between aggressiveness and initiative, I look at the fruit of the person's efforts. If the fruit is self-promotion, then ambitious aggression is probably at play. But if people genuinely are being helped and the ministry is growing, then initiative is more likely the spark.

In our church, I've met many businessmen who've achieved success by being shrewd and aggressive and working harder than anyone else. On the surface, they would seem to be good leadership candidates. But unless cunning individuals are submitted to the Holy Spirit and accountable to other leaders, they're like loose cannons on deck.

We place people like these under other strong leaders who can temper them. We've found that in time, the Holy Spirit can get hold of them and harness their self-will. The change usually appears first in how they treat their families or subordinates at work. Once the Holy Spirit directs their drive, they often show the makings of effective, godly leaders.

Leaders are judged, in part, by their selection of co-workers. Select the right people, and ministries thrive. Select the wrong people, and doors are opened to problems that stifle ministry and damage credibility.

What are the keys to wise selection? Time, prayer, and discernment. Jesus didn't choose the Twelve by walking along the seashore saying, "I want you and you and you. Drop your nets and follow me." In his first year of ministry, Jesus worked with a large number of disciples. When it was time to center in on potential leaders, he went away for a night of prayer, returned, and then selected the Twelve (Luke 6 and Mark 3).

If Jesus needed to wait a year and pray all night, shouldn't we wait to see the fruit of potential leaders' lives? Shouldn't we pray diligently for discernment? We kid ourselves if we think we can select wisely without going through the same careful process Jesus employed.

How to Work Through Others

After placing the right people in the right spots, we have to make critical decisions about which tasks to do ourselves and which to accomplish through them. Naturally, there are certain tasks we never delegate. Peter Drucker refers to those as a leader's "unique contribution," what he alone brings to the organization. Leaders shouldn't delegate what they are best positioned and gifted to accomplish.

A senior pastor, for instance, typically is gifted and trained as a teacher. Often his most significant contribution is teaching on Sunday mornings. So when he gets overloaded, he should focus on message preparation and delegate competing tasks to others.

My unique contribution at Willow Creek is to build our subministries. No one else is so commissioned to help our ministry directors develop their departments. Someone else can type my correspondence, lead singles meetings, or administrate our magazine, but no one else is called to oversee our department leaders.

How do we determine our unique contribution? By considering our gifts, passions, talents, background, personality, and temperament. Given that insight, we can then decide how we can best fulfill the requirements of our particular position.

I try to be a student of myself: Who did God make me to be? What has he called me to do? The best hours of my day should be given to make that contribution.

After I determine my slice of the circle, I need to look at the remaining tasks and ask, "Who can I find to help me complete the circle?" The key is to find people who feel about their slice the way I feel about mine.

For example, for a number of years I worked with our compensation committee. However, as the staff grew, the salary schedule became increasingly complicated. With no training in this area, I felt terribly inadequate. Yet technically, the responsibility fell in my circle.

At the time, a man in my small group was vice-president of personnel in a major corporation. His Ph.D. and vast corporate experience made salary negotiations a natural for him—and what's more, he enjoyed it.

Today he heads our compensation committee. Because of his expertise, our salary structure is worked out in great detail and everyone benefits. The staff is better served, the man gets to use his talents to help the church, and I am freed to do the tasks I do best. That happened because I found a leader who feels as strongly about compensation schedules as I do about ministry development.

After determining which tasks to do ourselves and which to delegate, we must decide how much responsibility to give and when to give it. At Willow Creek, we operate on this principle: Faithful with little, faithful with much. We start by giving people a small task or responsibility, and as they prove faithful in that, we give them more.

Sometimes seminary students call and say, "I need an internship. Can I teach at Willow Creek?" We always turn down offers like that. We might offer students the opportunity to lead a small group in their home, and if that works out, expand their leadership role. But we won't bestow great responsibility without a track record of faithfulness and effectiveness in our fellowship. "You start by speaking to five," we tell them, "and then we'll see about fifty."

We expect potential teachers to display strong character, evidence a robust spiritual life, and build relational credibility. Then, if their teaching gift is affirmed, we find a place for them in ministry. The same expectations help us determine what initial administrative or service roles to offer other possible leaders.

While we shouldn't give too much responsibility too soon, it's important to challenge those through whom we work. In fact, it may be more damaging to expect too little of our workers than too much.

Typically, people are drawn into leadership because others have noticed their competence in a variety of ways. Usually they're energetic, busy people who have proven they can do a job well. When people like this are bitten by the ministry bug, and when they taste the fulfillment of fruitfulness, they want to move ahead.

That's why it's so important to challenge them. To give them too meager a task, to expect too little, to fail to increase their responsibility at the proper time, is an insult. Competent people want to grow into positions of greater responsibility.

Naturally, I wouldn't expect someone who has never worked in children's ministry to assume a lead teacher role in Sunday school. I'd start such a person with a more manageable challenge, perhaps as a small-group leader. However, after a year or so, when the person's competence has been proven, I'd likely make him or her a lead teacher with twenty-five to fifty students.

It's necessary, of course, to talk with workers and monitor their progress. I can't dump a challenge on them and disappear. If I let colleagues down in their responsibilities, I'm not challenging them; I'm losing them.

Managers need to walk a fine line. They need to move people along at a reasonable rate so they don't feel overwhelmed. But they also need to remember that competent people usually feel most effective when they're stretched, when their responsibilities pull them a step beyond their comfort level. High-potential leaders would rather be roused by challenge than indulged by comfort.

It's that realization that keeps me on my knees. I need divine discernment to know how to challenge workers without overwhelming them.

I tend to be an optimist who sees the best in people and expects the best from them. I want to tell leaders, "You can do it. I know you can." But I can't say that to just anyone. So I don't glean leaders from whatever grows in the field. I prayerfully choose people who display character, spiritual maturity, and competence. Most often, people like that rise to the challenges of ministry.

The Payoff

Recently, circumstances forced me to act as interim director of one of our subcommittees. Because I already had a full slate of responsibilities, and because the subministry desperately needed a change, I had to find a strategy that would assure a quick turnaround. So I asked myself: *What is going to change this ministry most dramatically in the shortest time?* The answer was clear: key leaders. So I devoted my time and energy to finding potential key leaders.

Focusing on this A priority meant living with other problems, such as inadequate facilities and outdated curriculum. But I couldn't afford to tackle these problems at the cost of my primary task: finding key leaders.

For a while the ministry felt like a huge weight around my neck. Some days I went to the office at 4:00 A.M. because I couldn't sleep. I was exhausted, I wasn't giving my family what they needed, and the ministry was still in desperate need of change. At best, I was only propping it up.

The final turnaround came when we found the right person to head a major part of the department. The woman we called revolutionized the program. Her volunteers are now enthusiastic, and new people constantly are being attracted to the ministry. The entire program is functioning more smoothly, and details like facilities and curriculum can now be attended to.

Thanks to the contributions of the right leader, a major subministry has undergone a dramatic metamorphosis—and I have become a saner pastor and family man. Now I spend only one afternoon a week on that ministry, coordinating the efforts of the three new primary leaders. I have that luxury because I diligently pursued my A priority of finding leaders through whom I could work. I view that as a major accomplishment of my year.

Had I simply continued as a crutch for the ministry, both the ministry and I would still be limping along. But because I made it a priority to raise up leaders, we now have a healthy department.

When we build ministry that way, everybody wins.

3

Building Your All-Volunteer Army

*Instead of following the axiom "find a need and fill it," I
want to find and equip people first, then find the
ministry needs they can fill.*

—Ken Horton with Al Sibello

The lazy days of summer? Hardly. It's more like Panic City for
those of us who have to keep various ministries supplied
with workers.

When the preschool coordinator tells you no one is left to
teach the two-year-olds, what's a pastor to do? How do you answer the question, "Would it disturb the service that much if the
two-year-olds sat with their parents?"

Recruiting workers, always a challenge, is brought sharply
into focus during the summer, whether keeping ministry positions filled or gearing up for fall programs.

Once, in an attempt to staff our nursery, we resorted to
heavy-handed tactics, assigning parents to nursery duty on a
particular Sunday, whether they volunteered or not.

"If you've got kids in the nursery," we said in effect, "then
we expect you to carry your fair share."

Then we wondered why so many helpers failed not only to
show up for duty but failed even to come to church on their
assigned days. We discovered draftees often go AWOL without
completing their tour of duty. Such encounters have caused us
to rethink our entire approach to filling ministries in our church.

Though I've always paid lip service to the idea of helping people find a ministry geared specifically for them—a place where they can use their own gifts—I haven't always succeeded. Sometimes I've resorted to guilt, subtle manipulation, and cajoling—all for the sake of getting a yes.

I've learned, however, that's not enough. I can twist someone's arm and wrench a yes from between clenched teeth. But if I don't touch the person's heart, the commitment won't last. Those who are manipulated into service often serve with limited effectiveness. Who can blame them? I'm not enthused about being pressured either.

Trying to draft an army for the church doesn't work for the long haul. It's only when we begin enlisting people that their service changes from "ought to" motivation to "want to" motivation. And they're more likely to stay for the long term. We've discovered it's possible to create a climate where people want to serve.

Here are some of the ways we've shifted our approach.

Fill the Person, Not the Program

Needs are much easier to find than the people to meet those needs. I've learned that lesson the hard way.

When I develop a program before developing the people who serve, I often end up with trouble. So now I try to start with people and find the ministries they'd like to do.

We shifted the focus of our nursery from the need we had (taking care of infants and toddlers) to helping people find significance by serving others. Our nursery took on a whole new look. Now we don't have to force parents to serve their tour of duty. We have enough others who enjoy being part of our "Helping Hands" ministry: grandmothers, teenagers, even marrieds who are not yet parents.

We also encourage our people to experiment with different things until they discover the interests and gifts that belong uniquely to them.

Dean and Joanna started out working with youth. Increasingly, though, they found opportunities to help people—teens and adults—troubled by alcohol or drugs. Dean had been helped by a Twelve-Step program and wondered if he and Joanna couldn't lead a similar program in the church.

"We'd like to start a Christ-centered program," they told the church leaders, "that would help people overcome chemical abuse."

They were permitted to back out of youth ministry and step into another area, and that involved starting a new ministry. People took precedence over the program.

Dean and Joanna now lead a support group for people struggling with substance abuse and encourage dozens of people to overcome addictions with the help of Christ. Along the way, the church leaders have explored resources with them and encouraged them in their efforts. Some of Dean and Joanna's energies have expanded beyond our church and they have helped other churches start similar ministries.

Now, instead of following the axiom "find a need and fill it," I want to find and equip people first, then find the ministry needs they can fill.

Use Your Passion, Not Your Position

People respond to my heart more than my words. Because potential volunteers usually recognize what really motivates me, I shape my focus by several priorities.

Volunteers are leaders-in-training

I want to help people develop as leaders, not merely plug another leak in the ministry dike. My goal is to make *them* fruitful in ministry, not merely enlist them to help *me* do ministry.

Certainly, there are quicker methods to lining up volunteers. It takes time to model, explain, encourage, and release people into various leadership roles.

That's one reason why I work to link rookies with veterans

already involved in ministry. When volunteers work as apprentices alongside those who do ministry, they identify more with the person than the program. And because the heart is in the person, not the work, volunteers catch the passion for the ministry and acquire a sense of ownership for it.

Doyle is one volunteer who caught the vision and is now a leader. Seasoned over time, he's now widely recognized as one of our church's most gifted "pastors," though he is not officially on staff. In fact, he owns a sign-making business.

Doyle and his wife, Freddie, became believers after their children from previous marriages were adults. Later they faced several family traumas. Some relationships were severely strained. They suffered while watching their own children go through divorce. But through these difficult experiences, Doyle's heart grew more compassionate and tender. His natural concern for people deepened.

Now Doyle has several people working with him, helping in his ministry to hurting people. His team teaches and leads a dynamic adult fellowship every Sunday. He really is the front-line pastor for that group of adults. He works with the church staff, keeping us posted about ministry needs. We, in turn, encourage him with his work as he visits the sick and counsels the discouraged.

When one member of Doyle's group died, I worked with the family to prepare the funeral.

"Could Doyle have a part in the service?" they asked. "He's been such a help to our family; it seems only right that he help us through this as well."

Now when I face any pastoral care situation with someone from Doyle's group, I routinely ask, "Would you like Doyle to participate?" His ministry is informal but powerful.

I've noticed three benefits as I've encouraged volunteers to be leaders:

1. Their creativity is unleashed, improving their ministries.

2. Their commitment is strengthened because they feel more responsible for their own ministries.

3. Their confidence is developed as they experience God's blessings in their ministries.

Minister to the ministers

Our church leaders work hard to encourage our volunteers. When a volunteer faces a personal crisis or when ministry involvement begins disrupting someone's personal life, we want to focus on what is best for that individual.

Tim and Cheryl, who worked with our preschool children, found themselves facing several major crises. Tim unexpectedly lost his job. Then their infant son was diagnosed with microcephaly, an abnormality in the development of the brain. They were ministers who needed ministry themselves. We gave them time off from their teaching and offered personal support and encouragement as they worked through their difficulties.

At times, our commitment to encourage volunteers in tangible ways may mean we'll have to face short-term adjustments. Perhaps we'll have to curtail the ministry they've been doing altogether. It's a small price to pay. Ministry that harms the ones who do it ceases to be ministry; it does not honor God.

If we rigidly hold people to their commitments to serve, we can do irreparable damage to them and the work they've done. But if we minister to the ministers, they will grow stronger and in the long run be able to extend their own ministry.

Make others feel significant

One of the greatest sources of satisfaction is seeing people you've worked with move on to develop their own ministries. We encourage our leaders to make this their goal—to find their own spiritual fulfillment by seeing others develop a joyful, fruitful ministry.

To help our volunteers see this, I need to model this perspective in my relationships with other churches and ministries. If I cannot be thankful for what God does through others, I'll never be able to release our own volunteers to achieve their full potential. If I feel threatened by the accomplishments of a ministry colleague, for example, I set up a competition, though perhaps subtle and/or subconscious. Such an attitude undermines my own effectiveness. Personal insecurity can have a crippling effect on ministry.

A pastor who keeps looking over his shoulder at an up-and-coming associate will poison his own ministry and, at the same time, stifle the ministry of his associate. There is no joy or fulfillment where mistrust and insecurity color a relationship.

When the family first asked if Doyle could participate in the funeral service, I could have felt insecure: *Are they suggesting I can't handle it? What do they have against me? What can Doyle do better than I?* But if I had responded that way—even if I was able to mask my insecurities—Doyle wouldn't be the laypastor he is today. I would have been the lid on his potential.

Lately, I have frequently mentioned in public my appreciation for the other pastors and churches in our community as we prepare for a Luis Palau Crusade. Hearing my sentiments helps our volunteers learn something about the spirit of cooperation. When they see genuine enthusiasm from their pastor for what God is doing through others, they are more apt to find joy in releasing their own co-workers to other ministries in our church or community.

Be patient

Several years ago, we sensed a need for a divorce recovery group in our church. Several of our members had gone through painful separations. They wondered how they could pick up the pieces of a shattered marriage. Naturally, some came to the leaders of the church for help.

"Can you start a group that will minister to our needs?" they asked.

We actively explored various options, but it soon became clear that no one was available who had the necessary qualifications for such a ministry. We were frustrated because an obvious need was not being met. But we determined to be patient.

We wanted God to supply the right leadership. Forcing the

issue would only create additional problems as well as leave the issue of divorce recovery unmet.

Finally, after two years, God brought the right person along. Charlie had the spiritual, personal, and professional qualifications necessary to lead such a group. God's timing is often revealed when he motivates a person who has both the compassion and desire to minister.

Prayerful patience has an added value. Sometimes people suggest ministries that do not seem feasible. Working slowly through such suggestions enables us to treat each idea credibly, allowing them to take on their own life—or die a natural death.

A couple of years ago, during a change of leaders in our youth ministries, two moms of teenage girls wanted to teach a Saturday morning Bible study for sixth-grade girls. Their chosen subject was J. I. Packer's theological volume *Knowing God*. My initial response was "wrong time, wrong book."

But after we discussed my concerns, they still wanted to try it. So we went ahead. The result was a life-changing experience for twenty girls and two moms.

Of course, this approach also leaves the door open for failure. When Jim asked if he could start a counseling ministry or support group for those who felt stressed out, we supported his efforts. One of our elders joined with him to strategize how best to reach those who were, as Jim put it, "living on the edge."

Our prayers and encouragement, however, did not dictate that something tangible had to result from his concern and efforts. So when the necessary resource people and enthusiasm did not emerge, Jim's ministry for hurting people did not materialize. But he says he was strengthened in the process of planning for it and encouraged by how we validated him.

And someday the time may be right for that particular ministry to take off.

Serving Is a Privilege, Not a Plight

When I see ministry as a privilege, I am less inclined to force people into service. I want to be free of the compulsion to make people fit my agenda. Rather, I want our volunteers to experience the joy of developing their own aptitudes and calling.

This fundamental attitude shift makes a huge difference in the way we work with people. We're not recruiting; we're inviting people to grow.

We have found people need to give more of themselves to fewer commitments. That is, some people get involved in too many ministries and eventually turn sour because they can't give adequate energy and enthusiasm to any of them.

We ask people to focus on one major area of ministry. If a second area is wanted, it should be a minor contribution.

When each believer wholeheartedly gives himself or herself to one ministry that is honestly enhanced by that person's gifts, every vital ministry in our church and in our community will be fully staffed. The benefits of this principle have been substantial.

It helps us develop long-term ministry

One team of adults has now taught three-year-olds for more than ten years. They have enough people working together to allow occasional breaks for those who need some time off to be rejuvenated. And they have a sense of God's leadership, which makes their ministry fulfilling while at the same time challenging—considering it involves working with small children.

It frees the church staff

This approach releases our paid staff to focus more on planning and development of leadership. AWANA, a Bible memorization program for children, was struggling after two years of development. Although led by laypeople, Tim, our Christian education pastor, was constantly investing large amounts of time to keep the program going. Our elders decided that unless stronger lay leadership surfaced, we would cancel the program.

In the year of evaluation that followed, God placed more than ten AWANA leaders from other parts of the country in our church. It became obvious to us that God was working in this ministry. Five years later, with almost sixty leaders and 200 children involved each week, Tim has been able to back off, providing only basic oversight and encouragement.

It fosters a life-style of ministry

By focusing on who they are more than what they do, we remind people that they are serving God, not a church or a pastor. By emphasizing a direct sense of accountability to God, we hope to prevent volunteers from thinking of their ministries solely as a specific event or time. We want them to see all of life as an opportunity to serve.

We want our volunteers to feel the freedom of ministry empowered by the Holy Spirit. They understand that ministry within our church takes place with the guidance and encouragement of the elders and pastors. But they also know that the possibilities for what they can do are endless. God has lots of surprises for us. We now miss fewer of them because we've encouraged people to listen for God's direction in their lives.

When Carolyn finished Bible Study Fellowship's five-year program, she wondered if God could use what she had learned. Shortly afterward, she began to recognize the needs of her ninety-two-year-old mother. Though her mother still lived independently, she craved interaction and meaningful dialogue.

So did many of her mother's friends who lived in nursing homes. So Carolyn began to teach a Bible study at a local nursing home, taking her mother along with her. Now her ministry includes study groups in five nursing homes.

Carolyn initiated the program—prompted by the Spirit, not by the leaders of the church.

We highlight such stories in our congregation because we would like more of our church ministry to be Spirit-prompted, not pastor-pushed.

One of our elders reminds me often, "Be careful not to overmanage the work of God." We have learned to give God plenty of room to use people in ways we cannot imagine.

At times we still catch ourselves being tempted to twist someone's arm as we try to keep some church program afloat. But we have discovered it's better by far to focus on God's priorities, making ministry for both leaders and volunteers a joyful experience and a true privilege.

4

Turning Pewsitters Into Players

*If we broaden the opportunities for people to get
involved, potential leaders will begin to shine.*

—Marlene Wilson

What motivates a pewsitter to stay in the pew?
Many people in the church have professional or technical skills of some kind, yet are reticent to use them in the church. I've heard pastors say, "I know what this person does outside the church. But as soon as he enters these doors, it's as if he doesn't know a thing." This likely happens because the person feels he is on the pastor's turf in the church and tends not to want to usurp power. Unless he is asked to use his leadership skills, he will backpedal.

I was a member of one congregation for twenty years and another for eight years. Only once in each congregation was I asked to help train volunteers. I felt a great sadness because I know training is my gift. The mind-blowing thing of the new congregation I've joined is that they've already asked me to train.

In every church there are people who are ready to serve but who need help or an invitation to do so. To transform members from passive to active, I recommend the following.

1. *Identify and develop skilled people.*

I suggest developing an interview process for new members. Even if the church is small, the key is in talking about the possibilities.

In the interviews, the first questions to ask are

"What are your gifts and talents?"

"What do you like to do?"

The next questions are

"Has your experience with this congregation so far been good or bad?"

"Are there things you'd like to contribute to the church that you've never been asked to do?"

"Do you want more, less, or different involvement?"

"What are your dreams for this congregation?"

It is amazing what comes out of these conversations. People share things they've never shared before.

2. Correct the causes of burnout.

Not all people like being thought of as church leaders. Part of their resistance may be to the old model of leadership: They don't want to be at the church every time the doors are open.

Because of what they have experienced, the view that many have of leadership is of someone burning out. For example, why do churches have a hard time recruiting small-group leaders? Because to many people, leadership means "I've got to take over the whole thing." They think, *I don't have the time. I want to go where I can be fed.* Burnout is why a great many people who were pillars somewhere else are now pewsitters. They're not going to get used up again. They aren't saying yes to anything.

For this reason, churches need to redefine leadership from "How much have you done?" to "How many others have you involved?"

To further prevent people from getting used up, one key is to rethink the work in light of the gifts of the people. I want every team member to answer four questions.

1. What are the strengths I bring?

2. What are the weaknesses I bring?

3. What is my major concern for this group?

4. What is my major dream for this group?

Answer those questions, and the group will begin to know what each one is good at. Then they begin to think of themselves as a team, rather than one leader and a bunch of followers.

Of course, not every layperson should lead. In *Servant Leadership*, Robert Greenleaf said not everybody's gift is leadership and that being a good follower is as important as being a good leader. Some people don't want to be leaders, don't have the gift of leadership, and shouldn't be forced or talked into it.

If we broaden the opportunities for people to get involved, the potential leaders will begin to shine. Then they will need training. They need to know the qualities of a leader, how to work with difficult people, and how to lead in different situations.

3. Keep pillars from becoming obstacles.

Another obstruction to involving new people is the body of longtime volunteers who are accustomed to the way things have always been done. When I started training volunteers, I listened to those I call the "pillars," the 20 percent, saying, "We're so tired of doing everything ourselves. Why don't other people get involved?"

I listened. But when I helped implement new ways to recruit volunteers, the pillars wouldn't give up their hold on ministry!

Often, pillars are older. In many congregations, particularly smaller ones, their volunteerism is the only source of power they've ever had. To ask them to share their work is to ask them to share their power. And that is threatening.

If the pillars admit there is a problem—too few doing too much of the work in the church—the pastor must say, "We need to change the way we're doing things. We're losing people because they're burning out. Too many people are exiting the back door, and it may be because there's no meaningful place for them here. Let's at least look at some options."

4. *Change the "I" to "we."*

Some pastors say, "I don't have time for all this." The problem is the word "I." It assumes that if it's going to be done, it is the pastor who will do it.

It doesn't have to be this way. The first step is to analyze the makeup of the congregation. Many have several laypeople who could become involved in a project or ministry. The pastor could be part of the team but not necessarily its leader. This group would survey the congregation and assess what should be put into place, writing out the volunteer opportunities, talking to individuals, and evaluating current training for volunteers. The group then decides together with the pastor one or two priorities for the coming year.

Of course, there will always be more ministry needed than there will be workers to meet those needs. But if laypeople are being developed, the pastor will not so easily become overwhelmed with the enormous amount of work to be done.

PART 2

Selection

5

Spotting a New Leader

The best predictor of the future is the past.

—Fred Smith

The most gifted athletes rarely make good coaches. The best violinist will not necessarily make the best conductor. Nor will the best teacher necessarily make the best chair of the department. It is critical to distinguish between the skill of performance and the skill of leading the performance. They are entirely different skills.

It's also important to determine whether a person is capable of learning to lead. The natural leader will stand out. It is more difficult to identify those who are capable of learning the art of leadership over time.

Following are several traits to help determine whether someone is capable of learning to lead.

Ten Signs of Potential

1. *Leadership in the past.*

The best predictor of the future is the past. When I was in business, I took note of any worker who told me he was superintendent of a Sunday school or a deacon in his church or a Boy Scout leader. If he showed leadership outside of the job, I wanted to find out if he had some leadership potential on the job.

2. *The capacity to create or catch vision.*

When I talk to people about the future, I want their eyes to light up. I want them to ask the right questions about what I'm talking about.

The founder of Jefferson Standard built a successful insurance company from scratch. He assembled some of the greatest insurance people by simply asking, "Why don't you come and help me build something great?"

A person who doesn't feel the thrill of challenge is not a potential leader.

3. *The constructive spirit of discontent.*

Some people would call this criticism, but there's a big difference in being *constructively discontent* and being *critical.* If somebody says, "There's got to be a better way to do this," I can see if there's leadership potential by asking, "Have you ever thought about what that better way might be?"

If he says no, he is being critical, not constructive.

But if he says yes, he's challenged by a constructive spirit of discontent. That's the unscratchable itch. It is always in the leader.

People locked in the status quo are not leaders. I ask of a potential leader, *Do you believe there is always a better way to do something?*

4. *Practical ideas.*

Highly original people are often not good leaders because they are unable to judge their output; they need somebody else to say, "This will work" or "This won't work."

Brainstorming is not a particularly helpful practice in leadership because ideas need to stay practical. Not everybody with practical ideas is a leader, of course, but leaders seem to be able to identify which ideas are practical and which aren't.

5. *The willingness to take responsibility.*

One night at the end of the second shift, I walked out of the plant and passed the porter. As head of operations, I had started my day at the beginning of the first shift.

The porter said, "Mr. Smith, I sure wish I had your pay, but I wouldn't want your worry."

He equated responsibility and worry. He wanted to be able to drop his responsibility when he walked out the door and not carry it home. That's understandable, but it's not a trait in potential leaders.

I thought about the porter's comment driving home. If the vice-president and the porter were paid the same money, I'd still want to be vice-president. Carrying responsibility doesn't intimidate me because the joy of accomplishment—the vicarious feeling of contributing to other people—is what leadership is all about.

6. *The completion factor.*

I might test somebody's commitment by putting him or her on a task force. I'd find a problem that needs solving and assemble a group of people whose normal responsibilities don't include tackling that problem. The person who grabs hold of the problem and won't let go, like a dog with a bone, has leadership potential. This quality is critical in leaders because there will be times when nothing but his iron will says, "Keep going."

Dale Carnegie used to say, "I know men in the ranks who will not stay in the ranks. Why? Because they have the ability to get things done." In the military it is called "completed staff work."

With potential leaders, when the work comes in, it's completed. The half-cooked meal isn't good enough.

7. *Mental toughness.*

No one can lead without being criticized or without facing discouragement. A potential leader needs a mental toughness. I don't want a mean leader; I want a tough-minded leader who sees things as they are and will pay the price to see them through.

Leadership creates a certain separation from one's peers.

The separation comes from carrying responsibility that only the leader can carry. Years ago, I spoke to a group of presidents in Columbus, Ohio, about loneliness in leadership.

One participant, president of an architectural firm, came up afterward and said, "You've solved my problem."

"What's your problem?" I asked.

"My organization is always confused," he said, "and I didn't know why. Now I know it's because I don't like to be lonely; I've got to talk about my ideas to the rest of the company. But they never know which ideas will work, so everybody who likes my idea jumps to work on it. Those who don't, work against it. Employees are going back and forth—even when the idea may not materialize at all."

Fearing loneliness, this president was not able to keep his ideas to himself until they were better formulated. A leader must be able to keep his or her own counsel until the proper time.

8. Peer respect.

Peer respect doesn't reveal ability, but it can show character and personality.

Trammell Crow, one of the world's most successful real estate brokers, said that he looks for people whose associates want them to succeed. He said, "It's tough enough to succeed when everybody wants you to succeed. People who don't want you to succeed are like weights in your running shoes."

Maxey Jarmen used to say, "It isn't important that people like you. It's important that they respect you. They may like you but not follow you. If they respect you, they'll follow you."

9. Family respect.

I also look at the family of a potential leader. Do they respect him or her?

Fifteen years ago, my daughter said, "Dad, one thing I appreciate is that after you speak and I walk up, you are always attentive to me. You seem proud of me." That meant a lot to me.

If respect isn't there, that's also visible. At a church-growth conference, a well-dressed preacher approached me after I had spoken. A few steps behind him trailed his wife. With his chest swelling, he asked, "How would you like to come to my church and speak to a *thousand* people Sunday night?"

I couldn't resist saying, "I would have liked that in an earlier day, but I've given up speaking to smaller groups."

His wife's face lit up like a Christmas tree. Her body language revealed what she thought of her husband's egotism. The family's feelings toward someone reveal much about his or her potential to lead.

10. *The quality that makes people listen.*

Potential leaders have a "holding court" quality about them. When they speak, people listen. Other people may talk a great deal, but nobody listens to them. They're making a speech; they're not offering leadership. I take notice of people to whom others listen.

Four Final Checks

It's not enough for people to have leadership potential; they must have character and the right setting in which to grow. Before I give someone significant leadership responsibilities, I find it helpful to ask myself four questions:

- *What will this person do to be liked?* It's nice to be liked, but as a leader it cannot be the controlling factor. The cause must be the prime motivator.
- *Does this person have a destructive weakness?* There are only two things I need to know about myself: my constructive strength and any destructive weakness. A destructive weakness may not show up on a test; it's a character flaw. A destructive weakness may, for example, be an obsession. An obsession controls us; we don't control it. It only grows worse over time.

I met for a while with a gregarious former president of a corporation. He had recently lost his job. During our meetings, I kept saying to myself, *I can't buy this guy. There's something beneath the surface that doesn't ring true.* One of the last times he came to see me, in a burst of honesty he said, "Fred, I'm going to a psychiatrist."

I asked, "Do you care to tell me what it's about?"

He said, "I'm a congenital liar. I can't tell the truth."

Then I knew what had bothered me.

- *Can this person accept reasonable mistakes?* I recently had lunch with an accountant who works for a large accounting firm. He said, "I look at every page that passes through my department, but I'm finding that difficult, given the size of my department."

He is afraid of delegating and having someone make a mistake. But perfection is too expensive; employees can't live under that tyranny. A leader has to be able to accept reasonable mistakes—not repeat them but accept them. Failure is part of accepting leadership; you can't let it eat away at you.

- *Can I provide this person the environment to succeed?* It is so important, particularly in the early days of someone's leadership, that he or she be put into a congenial environment. I wouldn't want, for example, to place someone who requires mentoring with a leader who pays no attention to people.

An environment that threatens our sense of security or well-being splits our concentration from the cause. Young leaders need an environment in which they can concentrate on leading.

I once tried to get an employee in a small southern town promoted but without success. I was honest with him, saying I didn't think his future was in the company; I suggested he go out on his own. I felt he had potential. He eventually became president of the local bank. We still maintain contact.

Some of my most rewarding memories involve young people in whom I believed and shared in their promotion.

6

Recruiting Volunteers

*We need to look for ways to harness people's
dissatisfaction for ministry.*

—Leith Anderson

Most of the work of the local church is done by volunteers.
If the volunteers are ministering effectively, the church is
ministering effectively. If they're not, the church is not. It would
be difficult, therefore, to conceive of a pastoral responsibility
more important than helping volunteers be effective in their
ministries.

Working with volunteers in the church involves three basic
responsibilities: motivating people, guiding them to the right
ministry, and supporting and supervising them as they minister.

Motivating People to Minister

Motivation is not an arcane science. It begins with an understanding of people and what they need. As I have reflected
on that, I have developed a few guidelines for motivation within
the church.

Use gratitude rather than guilt

Guilt is probably the most powerful motivator in the church.
It's quick and effective. When people are desperate to get a job
done, they readily employ guilt.

But it also carries a high price tag: resentment. People motivated by guilt develop a subconscious hostility toward the leader and the institution. It is far better to motivate by appealing to gratitude—gratitude to God for all he has done.

I once attended a fund-raising banquet for the seminary from which I graduated. Before I walked in, I had my check made out. For me, at the time, the gift was substantial.

When the banquet host launched his appeal, he told how seven or eight faculty members were paid less than garbage collectors in New York City. (I remember thinking, *So what? Most people in this room are paid less than garbage collectors in New York City.*) His underlying message was, "You, the supporters of the school, don't pay the faculty enough." He was laying guilt on us.

I felt bad. I had wanted to give cheerfully. By the time he'd finished his speech, I had folded my check and put it in my pocket. I was sitting at the head table, but when the ice cream bucket came by, I didn't put in my check.

That host could have motivated by gratitude: "This faculty has had a great impact on your life. You're benefiting from them every day. You've got their books; you've got their lectures; you've got their example. God has blessed you through them. In response to the tremendous gift you've been given, you have an opportunity to say thank you."

If he would have said that, I probably would have ripped up my check and written one for a larger amount.

The same principle applies to motivating people to volunteer. Some time ago, because of some unusual circumstances that never should have happened, we didn't have an adequate number of Sunday school teachers for the fall program. Some people say that in that situation I should announce, "If somebody isn't going to teach the third graders, we won't have a third-grade class. The pupils can sit in Sunday school with their parents." It's tempting because it will work; somebody will volunteer. But the volunteer will be somebody who's already overloaded and probably not gifted to teach third graders. That's an awful approach to the Lord's work.

Even at a time like that, I want to say, "God has taught us wonderful things. He has richly blessed us. Here is a great opportunity God has given us to say thank you, to pass on his blessings to somebody else." That kind of appeal may not have an immediate effect, but for the long term it's much more effective.

Tap people's existing dissatisfaction

A satisfied need never motivates anyone. If you're totally satisfied, you won't get up in the morning. Before you can be motivated to do anything, you must be dissatisfied. The wonderful thing about the church is that within it there is always an adequate supply of dissatisfaction.

One person is dissatisfied by the loss of identity in a society that treats him more and more like a number. The church can say, "Here is a chance for you to be a significant person in a ministry." Another person is dissatisfied with the church facilities. That becomes a motivation for her to help plan for new facilities.

Our church has an abundance of leaders, and some people are dissatisfied because they want more opportunity to lead. We can say, "Do you want to run things? If you have those skills, great! We'll start another church for which you can provide the leadership." We need to look for ways to harness people's dissatisfaction for ministry.

Give volunteers more than they put in

This could be terribly misunderstood, but the main thing that keeps volunteers motivated is the sense they are getting more out of their service than they are putting into it. If they reach the point where they perceive they are giving more than they're getting, they will quit.

Teachers often say, "I get more out of the class by teaching it than I could by sitting and listening to the lesson." People volunteer so they can experience personal growth, find the satisfaction of serving God, become part of a significant organization, or enjoy camaraderie with other workers. For example, Sunday school teachers hold departmental meetings that they think are designed primarily to plan for the next quarter. But the main purpose of the meeting is to say to teachers, "When you're alone teaching six kids, really you are not alone. You're part of a team. If you become sick or go on vacation, somebody else will take over." The feeling of camaraderie the teachers take from these meetings gives them motivation to continue.

Even if a task involves pain or frustration, when people feel they are gaining spiritually from it, they will continue to serve. This means that you can expect a lot from people as long as you "pay" them a lot.

Several years ago our church held a consultation with Lyle Schaller. As part of it, we scheduled a board meeting for one o'clock on Friday afternoon. Although all the board members work on Friday afternoon, everyone was there. Afterward, Schaller commented that having everyone attend wasn't typical. I had never considered the possibility that anybody wouldn't come. I expected the board members to do whatever they had to do—take vacation, if necessary—to be there.

They are willing to do that, however, because their pay is high. Those board members consider board meetings the highlight of their month. In addition, throughout the year, we hold game nights at my house for the elders and their families. If an elder calls, he gets through immediately. I might not change my schedule for somebody else's wedding, but when elders' kids get married, I'm there. I build my life around them and give them preferential treatment, and they know it.

Volunteers' performance remains high when their pay remains high.

Rules for Recruiting

The church has a long history of using people to meet institutional needs. Not only is this approach disrespectful, but it also destroys motivation. Many churches are now learning to reverse the process, to begin not with the institution's needs but with the individual's gifts. Instead of saying, "We need a nursery worker for the fifth Sunday of the month," congregations are learning to ask, "Where should you be serving Jesus Christ?" With this approach, people become better matched to their responsibilities.

Admittedly, this takes time. Wooddale has established a policy that people cannot be asked to serve until their names have been cleared through the staff. This means most of our staff meeting is spent talking about where people can be deployed in ministry. If no one on staff knows a particular person, a staff member will meet with that person and discuss his or her spiritual development and interests.

Although this approach takes time, it protects people. One volunteer, for example, was urgently needed in our music program. However, after a pastor visited the home, he reported to his staff, "This couple has tensions in their marriage. The commitment to rehearsals wouldn't be good for them right now; they need the time at home." We respected that and determined to find somebody else or shut down that part of the music program.

Frankly, people respond better to an invitation when they discover it comes only after careful consideration by the staff. Suppose, for example, a person is gifted both in music and in working with teens, but because he's starting a new business, he doesn't have time to work in both areas. If we decide the greater need is in youth ministry, the youth pastor would explain to this person that he had been considered for another area as well but is being asked to take on only one responsibility at this time. Volunteers recognize this as interest in them as individuals.

We also offer a Human Resources Program that consists of a seminar, some tests, and an interview with a person skilled in personnel management. The program helps people identify their interests and gifts and to look for ways they can use them in the church.

For some reason, people are willing to admit they have almost any gift except evangelism. To determine who has that gift, we go to an adult Sunday school class—fifty to ninety people who know each other reasonably well. We ask everyone to write down names of people in the group who have the gift of evangelism. Usually, about ten names are repeated. Then a pastor can approach these ten people and say, "The people who have prayed and studied with you, those who know you best, say that you have the gift of evangelism. Would you like to develop that gift and use it more?"

Finally, before a person is approached about a position, a job description is developed that outlines the qualifications, relationships, and responsibilities, including term of service. This again helps people determine if the position is right for them.

Recruiting works better when the invitation comes not from some full-time church recruiter but from a person involved in that very ministry. Then the invitation is not, "Will you do this job?" but rather, "Will you join me in doing this job?"

In addition, we work hard to recruit well in advance of the assignment's starting date. Recruiting Sunday school teachers for the fall shouldn't take place in August; it should happen in April. This shows respect for volunteers and gives them time to think and pray about the commitment. The carefully considered commitment is much stronger than the one made hastily.

Normally, a person's first assignment in the church is small. We would never, for example, ask someone to teach an adult congregation if we had not first seen the person teach as a substitute. When we have broken this rule and have guessed incorrectly about a person's ability, we have lost people from the church. Removing people from a position causes them to lose face and to feel they need to find another congregation.

Of course, no matter how thoroughly we do these things, some placements won't work. Sometimes a person will say, "I've tried this for six months, but it's not my gift." When that happens, we need to say, "Fine. Then what should your ministry be?"

Targeting the "Epaulet People"

When there aren't enough volunteers to staff a program, leaders need to ask, "Is this something we shouldn't be doing?" Theologically, we assume that God will never expect us to do something for which he will not provide the resources. If the resources aren't there, we need to ask, "Should this be dropped?"

The answer lies, in part, in whether the ministry is essential. At Wooddale, for example, morning worship, Sunday school, and child care would be seen as essential. People expect these basic programs in a contemporary American church, so we would not allow these areas to go unstaffed.

But when we didn't have enough men for the men's choir, we dropped the choir. Wooddale organized a ten-kilometer run to increase visibility and outreach in the community, but when we didn't have enough volunteers anymore, we cut the program. These we can live without. Sunday school we cannot.

In addition, some volunteer roles are critical to the life of the church. One is a role I call "the introducer." This person instinctively knows how to connect a visitor with another person, and then he or she moves on to find the next visitor. This person tends to wander through the halls, and we forgive him or her for not coming to worship services. It is important to not tie up the congregation's introducer in teaching Sunday school. Growth depends on having one or more introducers free to do their work.

Other people I look for are the "epaulet men." On the eve of the Battle of Saratoga in 1778, Daniel Morgan led his Morgan's Rifles against the British army led by Gentleman Johnny Burgoyne. Morgan compared his troops and ammunition to the strength of the British, and it was obvious his Rifles were going to lose the battle. So the night before the battle, Morgan gath-

ered his men and said, "Don't waste your shot on those who
fight for sixpence a day. Aim for the epaulet men"—the officers
who wore insignia on their shoulders.

The next day, Morgan's Rifles went into battle. When they
had a private in their sights, they didn't pull the trigger. They
waited until they saw an epaulet man. Following this strategy,
Morgan's Rifles won the Battle of Saratoga, and some historians
say that it was the determining battle of the Revolutionary War.

In the church, we also win or lose by determining who
wears the epaulets. If we recognize the leaders and nurture
them, all the privates will line up behind them.

Corporate Ethos

In most churches, the pastor cannot possibly monitor every
volunteer position. How, then, can a pastor hope to ensure that
people are performing well and conscientiously?

The first and most important thing a pastor does is establish
the corporate ethos. Pastors can't manage every person, but
they can manage the corporate atmosphere, which in turn will
govern those people. Leaders can create an atmosphere that is
upbeat, biblically based, and rooted in prayer. They can set a
climate that includes making proposals before you do things,
being accountable, and not operating unilaterally. Those principles come to be understood throughout the organization.

How is this ethos created? By the way the pastor relates to
the people he or she supervises directly. These people, in turn,
treat others the way they have been supervised, and the approach ripples through the organization.

I try to demonstrate to those I supervise that I'm there to
serve them. After board meetings, for example, which may go
until midnight or one o'clock in the morning, I stay with one or
two other people and clean the room. I want to serve that
board, so I clean the room, meaning they can get home earlier.
And I want to serve the church custodian. One time a custodian
said to me, "The board sure leaves the room a mess." Now I

clean the room so he doesn't have a mess the next morning. My hope is that these people will say, "If the pastor will do that for me, I'm going to do that for other people."

Patterns like these eventually duplicate themselves in the organization. For example, our pastors for junior high students and senior high students serve their volunteers so well that they have a waiting list of people to serve.

I never want a volunteer at Wooddale to be recruited and then abandoned. I know that if someone asks a teacher, "Will you teach next year?" but has not talked with that teacher all year long, the teacher will not do it. The only way I can hope to avoid that is to create a corporate ethos that says, "Ongoing support is essential." And I can create that ethos only by continually supporting those people I directly supervise.

7

Recruitment's Missing Link

*One spiritual gift stands crucial to activating all the
others: the gift of administration.*

—Carl F. George

For a long time, volunteer behavior in the church was a mystery to me. My personal breakthrough in understanding came in phases. I had pastored University Baptist Church in Gainesville, Florida, for more than ten years when, one day, I went to a community meeting sponsored by a local hospital. Afterward, the doctor who had led the discussion was having coffee, and one of the matrons engaged him in animated conversation.

At one point he paused thoughtfully and asked a searching question: "What do you suppose motivates you to give your time and energy to this work?" He had discerned her to be a volunteer, and he wanted to estimate how her abilities might be applied to his program.

Several years later, that scene flashed in my mind as I stood in our church auditorium and listened to a young woman with glowing eyes and vivacious voice describe her recent visits to sick people in the hospital. She was bringing yet another group of names of patients she had encountered by word-of-mouth referral in the community, trying to schedule me to give these people the pastoral care she knew they would appreciate.

The love on her face as she recounted the details of her visits contrasted sharply with my own internal heaviness. For me, hospital visitation was a wearying chore. Carrying a heavy burden of administration, it seemed to me that there would always be more sick and dying people than I would have strength to minister to. Even the deathbed conversations and the remarkable appreciations expressed by patients and their families did not prevent me from dreading another set of hospital assignments.

She talked on, and my mind wandered to the earlier scene of the doctor questioning the volunteer. I said, half out loud, "What is it that motivates you to go to the hospitals to show mercy and extend comfort to these people?" Before the words were fully out of my mouth, I realized the source. "You have a gift of mercy!" I exclaimed. "God has given you a gift for consoling those in sorrow and comforting those in fear. You get such satisfaction from this that instead of a hospital call being an interruption, it's the highlight of your day! You find time to go to the hospital as eagerly as some people seek out an ice cream shop, don't you?"

"Yes, I get a great deal of joy out of doing this," she responded.

Then, my understanding growing as we talked, I said, "You must be affirmed in this gift of yours; you must know that God has called you to this. I want to pray with you now for a greater impact and effectiveness as you develop this ministry further." I went on to explain to her how to pray and read Scripture with the sick, how to minister to them herself without raising an expectation that I would follow up. She requested counsel on how to deal with some of the basic spiritual needs of these patients.

I left that pastorate shortly afterward to come to the Charles E. Fuller Institute, not yet fully understanding how God unfailingly gives gifts to his people, and that those gifts form the basis for all well-motivated, spiritually effective volunteer work. In retrospect, I realize a number of persons in the congregation had the same gift, and it was showing up in a similar way. They were projecting their gift onto me and assuming I would be as motivated to minister mercy and comfort as they were.

My failure to recognize their gifts meant we did not develop nearly as adequate a visitation program to the sick and hospitalized as we could have because I was unable to see what God was doing. He would have preferred for us, in a community with four major medical facilities, to develop this as a significant regional outreach. Since no church I knew of had such a program, no models were available. An adequate concept of gifts could have helped me understand that the availability of gifted workers is one way to detect God's guidance for programs of outreach or nurture.

It is my conviction that volunteer work in the church is more greatly enabled by spiritual-gift theology than by any other single factor, training technique, or conceptual base. And one spiritual gift stands crucial to activating all the others: the gift of administration.

Automatic Appraisers

As my fellow researchers and I have come to understand it, the administrator gift excels at clearly stating major and supporting goals, visualizing the division of labor required to enable a group to work together toward those goals, and especially appraising the work force: Who can handle which assignments? Another way to say this is that *an essence of the administrative gift is the ability to recognize ability.*

In our experience, administrators do not have to be asked to assess people's capabilities—they do it automatically. They are continually sizing up talent and have a rich store of observations from their contact with people around them. They carry in their memories a knowledge base. They can estimate skill in handling both supervisory functions and specific tasks.

We have also learned that laypeople with the gift of administration are typically very busy, employed in business or other positions where their gifts are utilized. Unfortunately, they often cannot help their congregations because their abilities have not been recognized or, if recognized, have not been requested. At the same time, they generate frustration in others by turning down any number of specific tasks in the church. Why? They know instinctively that they will not make maximum contributions in such slots; they have chosen to avoid non-administrator assignments.

We have rarely heard of a case where administrators were not willing to make room in their busy lives to do the things for which they had been uniquely, specially gifted. But they do not stand around casually, waiting to be asked. That isn't their style.

The Hash Position

Many pastors have leadership gifts. They have the ability to cast a vision of a desired future, to promote ideas, and to inspire people to enter into programs of committal or self-improvement. They regularly challenge, comfort, instruct, and correct. These elements of the leadership gift cause people to gain a sense of hope and destiny and to be willing to contribute their energies and money to the work of the church.

Unfortunately, many of these bright, capable, loving, energetic leader types do not have the insights needed to take the resources they have attracted and relate them to one another or to church goals. They can neither accomplish the goals nor bring satisfaction to the volunteer workers who are enlisted.

This is no cause for embarrassment. It is simply a proof of Paul's teaching that "there are different kinds of gifts" (1 Cor. 12:4), each of them distributed as the Spirit wishes. One of those gifts is *leadership* (Rom. 12:8). Another of those gifts is *administration* (1 Cor. 12:28). The two are not the same at all.

In working closely with hundreds of pastors in dozens of denominations, we have discerned that relatively few have the gift of administration among their dominant gifts. This has profound impact upon their ability to identify and direct volunteer workers within their congregation.

The absence of the administrative gift shows up sometimes

in the poor placements pastors make. At other times, it is seen in their inability to visualize a job description or position required to support their objectives. One of the most sure indicators is the creation of what we have come to call the "hash" or "dump" position on the church staff. Sometimes it is the second professional position, sometimes the fourth or fifth. Whatever its rank, it comes about when the pastor who lacks an administrative gift appraises all the weaknesses or problems of the church at a particular time, lumps them together into a job description, and employs the first available person who is naïve enough to think he or she could possibly fill the position. Hash positions may include everything from long-range planning to custodial work, with youth recreation and senior citizen counseling thrown in for good measure.

Regrettable War

Meanwhile, the tension between leadership-gifted pastors and administration-gifted laypeople (and/or staff) grows. C. Peter Wagner has commented in *Your Spiritual Gifts Can Help Your Church Grow* that Christians tend to project their spiritual gifts onto others. That is, they tend not to be aware of their own abilities as gifts, assuming that all other persons have the same potential.

Believe it or not, one of the easiest ways to identify a person's giftedness is to examine what he or she criticizes! One thing an administrator surely knows how to do is spot the absence of administrative performance in other people. However, in our observation, he rarely realizes that his pastor might not have the gift of administration. He assumes the opposite and then criticizes the pastor for laziness, unwillingness to delegate, lack of confidence in lay leadership, distrust of newcomers, backwardness, or unwillingness to manage intentionally. If he were in the pastor's position he would surely handle matters differently. The only excuses he can think of for the pastor are lack of humility, dedication, spirit, or commitment. These malignings are easy to radiate and difficult to overlook.

The pastor is naturally hurt by these criticisms and frequently launches a defensive action. How a leader wages war against administrators may take several forms.

- He may devalue the administration gift and consider matters like planning, goal-setting, monitoring, controlling, and supervising to be mere details, unworthy of serious consideration by the truly spiritual.
- He may insist that there are enormous differences between the business work and the church, and the body of Christ does not admit to the same kinds of intentional activity for which successful businesses are known.
- Pastors who are skillful in maneuvering can occasionally close out the business and administratively trained people from having any particular say, either at the church board or department leadership level.

Where the leader's defenses are successful, administratively gifted laypersons start compartmentalizing—turning off their brains and gifts at the door, having learned that to attempt to offer insights from their business life will only raise defensiveness from the minister and other leaders. This effectively blocks them from applying their gifts.

Loyal Legion

Other members of the church, however, seem much less problematic. Every pastor has, in varying numbers, a loyal legion of fans who comes to the rescue each time there is a call for help. Although church leaders have noted that relatively few people volunteer on a general call (pulpit announcement, bulletin insert, even costumed skit portraying worker needs), the ever-willing group is different. It is commended by the minister and frequently affirmed with mottoes like "The best ability is availability."

This motto, like other old wives' tales, needs to be carefully examined. Perhaps it should be rephrased to read, "The best ability (for a particular task) is the ability required to satisfactorily perform (that task)." If the need is for an emergency warm body with a good attitude, then availability may be the ability that wins the day. We have found, however, that many ministers do not recognize the gifts of availability for what they really are.

We have come to believe that the gifts of helps and service have as a key ingredient the willingness to be available to call for help. (Somewhat arbitrarily, it has been suggested that the gift of *helps* focuses on assistance to a person or persons, while the gift of *service* describes willingness to invest time and energy in a group or organization.) These long-suffering, service-gifted persons spend many hours in front of computers or with brooms in their hands or rearranging chairs or addressing and mailing envelopes or telephoning or doing multitudes of other things required for organizational maintenance.

If, when the call for volunteers goes out, those who respond have as part of their gift mix both helps or service *and* an additional gift that happens to match the task, the results can be positive. Suppose the youth department needs a substitute teacher. The loyal legion says, "We'll help." If one of them is accepted and appointed, and if he or she also happens to have a gift of exhortation, teaching, pastoring, or leading, the result is a happy combination.

Frequently, however, a "willing" worker is put into the teaching position but, failing to have the gift of teaching, burns out in a very short time. A variation occurs when the poorly performing helper, held to the task by continued pleas, eventually weakens the class to the point that its vitality is gone and its growth potential blighted. An administrator would define this as a case of improper volunteer placement based on failure to perceive gifts.

Ministers tend to misread availability as a spiritual virtue—that is, "willingness" or "loyalty," when, in fact, it is essentially an evidence of the gifts of helps or service.

Why are helping-gift people so available? Because many of

them tend not to stay with any assignment for a very long time. An element of their gift is to clear their agendas of obligations. Either they accept tasks of short duration, or else they drop longer assignments midstream. They are often short-haul workers whose enthusiasm for a particular job remains only as high as their sense that the organization really needs them for that phase of its work.

So now the problem can be seen more clearly: A minister with leadership gifts but without administrative insight seldom recognizes ability and thus perceives willingness as the helping gifts. The willing are assigned instead of the able.

What Leaders Can Do

The pastor with the gift of leadership is in a most strategic place. Through the power of the pulpit, he interprets not only Scripture but the history of the congregation as well. This power guides the church to set forth suitable goals for its ministry.

After that, the ability *to recognize, to affirm, and to enlist administrators* is crucial if those dreams, ideals, and visions are to become realities. Here are some steps to follow:

1. *Study the subject of spiritual gifts in depth.*

Naturally, I am partial to the writings of my friend and colleague C. Peter Wagner on the subject, but others have written instructively as well. Come to a sincere belief that it is okay not to have all the gifts.

2. *Learn to recognize people's gifts from their criticisms and suggestions.*

Determine to get *help* from each gift instead of a headache. Criticism is an opportunity to discover someone.

3. *Make it a practice to affirm the gifts you see.*

Verbalize that here is another gracious bequest of the Holy Spirit. This will raise your own awareness—and the other person's as well.

4. *Ask for help in the church according to gifts discerned.*

You may be surprised at the responses you get, because the Spirit implants a sense of stewardship in gift-holders and requires them to take seriously requests in line with their gifts. The transaction is suddenly not only two-way (between pastor and parishioner) but triangular.

5. *Enlist those with the gift of administration to serve on personnel and nominating committees, where they can practice making appointments by gift.*

Such people have a good sense of who can do what. They readily appreciate the usefulness of systems for discovering spiritual gifts, such as the Trenton Plan or the Modified Houts Questionnaire published by the Charles E. Fuller Institute. These tools help apply people according to their Holy Spirit-given gifts to the various offices of the church.

6. *Ask people individually how they see your gifts as helping them.*

It is useful to say, "What do you need from me in order to do your work?" This casts the person in the proper role of being responsible to minister. But it is even better to say, "What needs for help do you have that my gifts can meet?" This opens them up to the radical thought that you don't have all the gifts—and so they should not expect you to.

All of the above help to set a good atmosphere in which defensiveness recedes and ministry advances. A final suggestion for leaders:

7. *Keep spotting the gifts of administration by noting those who enjoy accomplishing things through others.*

These will be the people who can listen to your declarations of vision and then

- frame supporting strategies (often in writing);
- identify the individual tasks that comprise the strategies;
- visualize the job descriptions to cover the tasks;
- discern suitable people to fill the job descriptions.

What Administrators Can Do

We have interviewed dozens of frustrated laypeople and staff members with gifts of administration and have found a recurring attitude in almost all of them: They've given up on their pastors. They have concluded that the minister is an incurable impediment to progress, and therefore they can only sit and stew.

Three things administrators need to understand are

1. *The pastor is caught in a position that demands he be something of a star.*

This expectation is not necessarily of his own making, but it is a reality nonetheless. And there is no way he can delegate this role to someone else.

2. *Pastors who do not understand the difference between leading and administering generally do not know how to ask administrators for help.*

The words and concepts are simply not a part of their conscious thinking until they do some study in the area of spiritual gifts.

3. *Other people don't see what administrators see.*

The administrators' degree of giftedness is often unrecognized, so that they impute their insights to the pastor and are perplexed that he doesn't respond to "the obvious."

Administration-gifted people must discipline themselves to use their gift *for* the body of Christ rather than *on* the body of Christ. Careful language will go a long way to reduce defensiveness. Few pastors will refuse the person who asks, "Can I help you construct some supporting strategies for your vision? Can I help you find the people to make your dream happen?"

People-Based Building

When pastors and layleaders examine the parts of the body the Holy Spirit has given them, they can then imagine prayerfully what the presence of those individuals should mean in shaping and forming the congregation. This is quite different from the widespread approach to volunteer work, which says, "We have determined our goals and organization form. Now our staffing tables call for X number of workers for existing programs and Y number for new programs."

Congregations that grow as organisms—that is, with respect to the spiritual gifts of the people—are flexible, resistant to burnout, and confident that they are discovering the will of Christ. They are deploying the members of his body in ways that are satisfying, effective, and result in the production of both new converts and additional leaders in greater numbers than churches that are merely organizations.

8

When Is a Broken Person
Ready to Lead?

*If a person can't build deep friendships that
include accountability, that person is not ready
to lead in the church.*

—Daniel Brown with Bob Moeller

A man who recently joined our fellowship came out of the Jehovah's Witnesses. Three months after his conversion, his daughter died. Then the woman he had been dating broke off their relationship.

As if that weren't enough, his business collapsed; it's now half of what it used to be.

Today, this man comes to three services on Sunday. He can't seem to get enough of God. He's obviously not ready for significant leadership right now. But he's on the way toward the healing that could one day make him a powerful servant leader.

When will that be?

I don't know for sure. The goal is not to get him well enough so he can get on with the real business of the church. He *is* the real business of the church. But as his brokenness heals, his potential for leadership rises.

Knowing when a broken person is ready to lead can be difficult to determine. So is knowing how to ease them back into responsibility. Here's what I've learned.

Five Tests to Measure Leadership Readiness

I use five tests to measure whether someone is ready for responsibility.

1. *Are they honest with themselves?*

Recently, a former Navy pilot stood in a meeting and said that his charter-flying business had gone bust. He'd lost everything—his planes, his income, his dream.

He told us how he had struggled with bitterness and disillusionment until someone at church made an offhand comment: "The reason God can't do anything miraculous in your life is because you want to control everything."

That bracing remark started him on a genuine soul-search. He admitted to the Lord that "This whole thing has been about me and my goals for my life." He asked for God's forgiveness.

This story shows the pilot's true spirit. I can work with broken people who recognize they're broken. People who can't admit their sin, though, make me nervous. This pilot is now on a trajectory toward becoming a cell group leader.

2. *Are they in community?*

Several years ago a man applied for a staff position at our church. He possessed a number of spiritual gifts, including an uncanny insight into what God was doing in a person's life (what some call "a word of knowledge").

Before hiring him, I told him, "If you're going to help people, you've got to be in relationship with them. Otherwise, you'll never convince them you're only an ordinary guy working for an extraordinary God."

I sensed he was balking. I recommended he offer training in discerning God's will from the Scriptures to a cell group. Then I said, "Why don't you go out to dinner with the leader of the cell group. You two need to establish a friendship."

His face reddened. "Look, I'm fifty-one years old," he said. "What I want to do is ministry. I don't have time to waste on anything as frivolous as building relationships."

"Then you won't minister at this church," I replied.

He had failed an essential test of leadership. Community is essential to biblical leadership. If a person can't build deep friendships that include accountability, that person is not ready to lead in the church.

3. Will they labor in obscurity?

Katherine has the poise and stage presence of Snow White. As worship leader, she was almost too perfect. While never flashy in her song leading, people began to stumble over her flawlessness. My concern was people were beginning to think of her more as an image than as a real person.

I asked her, "Katherine, why don't you do something other than sing in the services for a while? Maybe you could work the sound board or something like that."

She intuitively understood my concern.

"That's a super idea," she said. She took a job out of the public eye.

Now after months of working in obscurity, she and her husband eventually became our worship leaders.

I no longer worry about Katherine's stage presence; I know she doesn't have to be front and center in worship.

A person isn't ready to lead until he or she is ready to disappear, to accept an obscure position and find fulfillment in that unseen role.

4. Are they flexible?

One of our associate pastors tended to overreact to people when he felt threatened. Often his defensiveness would cross the line into belligerence. I had been patient with him for years, but by allowing him to be pushy with people, I risked communicating to our congregation that it's okay to be brusque and rude with people if you're a spiritual leader.

The situation was complex, but as a direct result of this problem, I asked him to resign.

The rest of the story is that I asked the church leadership to participate in his restoration. We hired him back as soon as we fired him—but as an assistant pastor, not an associate. His secretary and some of his perks as associate were taken away. Today, he's becoming more flexible and patient with those he serves.

5. *Are they faithful in little?*

Jesus said, "If you've been faithful in little, then you will be made master of much." I view readiness to lead as a process. It begins months and years earlier when people are asked to do something as simple as pass out bulletins. Once they're found faithful doing that, we move them to something more demanding.

I recently told a woman who works on our staff, "In my mind, I actually hired you about three years before you came on staff."

She looked at me quizzically. "What do you mean?"

"I decided to hire you after I watched you and your husband carry those big silver coffeepots up and down the hallway week after week. No one else knew what you were doing, but I saw how eagerly you took on the task. That's when I decided you were someone we needed on our staff."

Four Steps to Responsibility

A woman whose husband left her (and the ministry) recently began attending our church. Shattered, she is casting about for emotional moorings to help her regain equilibrium. With a ministry background, she knows how to minister to people; she simply doesn't know how to do so in the midst of her pain.

Every follower of Christ is in some continual process of restoration; everyone is messed up and in need of God's healing. But at certain stages of our brokenness, we're not able to serve others. How can I help this woman back into leadership? I see the process in four stages.

1. *Love, without much advice.*

Personal disasters usually bring a person to the point of asking, "Does anyone care about me?" So I begin by saying, "I care about you, and so does God."

2. *Invite people to "little involvements."*

These don't call for much emotional fortitude and don't put people on the line. If people can't finish the job, it won't be a disaster. The service may be as simple as cutting out paper figures for our children's program or joining a crew to cut up a tree that came down during a windstorm.

3. *Help people understand their deep hurt about what has happened to them.*

I can't say, "Hey, get over this. It was no big deal." What registers as 2.0 on someone's emotional Richter scale may be a 9.0 for more sensitive souls. I try to help them accept the fact that there's nothing wrong with feeling deeply—actually, it's how God gifted them.

4. *Welcome people back to significant service—with permission to still carry their bruises.*

Spiritually speaking, I like to see if I can get a person with a broken arm to work with someone with a broken leg.

PART 3

Training

9

Equipping the Saints to Lead

*Training the board is one of the most effective ways to
increase unity and efficiency.*

—Larry Osborne

When Tim entered the ministry, he honestly looked forward to working with board members. Even though he'd heard his share of war stories, he figured his case would be different. As long as good people were elected and carefully discipled, he saw no reason why he and the board couldn't get along famously.

But five years later, as I talked with him, Tim wasn't so sure. Instead of partners, the board members seemed like adversaries. It no longer surprised him when even his best ideas were rejected outright. Sometimes he wondered if his board members understood ministry at all.

Odds are, they didn't.

They were sharp people and good leaders, but no one had trained them for their role. They had never been exposed to the unique principles and requirements of leading a spiritual and volunteer organization like the church. That was left for Tim and his fellow professionals to learn at Bible school and seminary. The layleaders were expected to figure it out on their own.

Tim's training, and their lack of it, caused them to view issues from radically different perspectives. They were suffering from what I call "educational separation." And with every new book Tim read and every seminar he attended, he slowly widened the gap between the way he saw the church and the way his layleaders did.

When Tim told me about his predicament, I understood. Early in my ministry, I had faced a similar situation. It seemed the more I learned about ministry the more I found myself frustrated with board members who had never been exposed to the material, much less sold on it.

Overcoming Educational Separation

Searching for some way to close the gap, I decided to set up an on-the-job training program to expose our board members to the same insights and principles I had been exposed to during my own training for ministry. But instead of focusing on the standard biblical and doctrinal themes, I zeroed in on practical theology, the stuff I studied in my pastoral ministry and Christian education classes.

Almost immediately, the gap in our perceptions of ministry began to close. Now that they were being trained like pastors, many of our board members started to think like pastors. Even when we disagreed, we had an easier time understanding and appreciating each other's viewpoint. Most important, we made better informed and wiser decisions.

Over the years, we've tackled a variety of subjects: church growth, educational theory, group dynamics, management styles, and the role of New Testament elders, to name a few. We've read articles and books by Lyle Schaller, C. Peter Wagner, Frank Tillapaugh, and others; and we've reviewed the insights of secular books such as *In Search of Excellence* and *Megatrends*. Also, whenever I or a staff member have attended a seminar or conference, we've summarized for the board any significant insights.

Training the board makes a difference—a big one. It's one of the most effective ways to increase unity and efficiency. Unfortunately, most board members receive, at best, a cursory introduction to their task.

In this chapter I want to look at the big picture: why training is so important and what principles guide the way I train.

Biblical and Practical Priorities

From my perspective, training board members should be a top priority for both biblical and practical reasons. First, the Bible mandates it. Ephesians 4:11–13 is a case in point. This popular text can be found on bulletin covers, letterheads, and logos. It articulates the Christian leader's responsibility to equip the rest of the body to do the work of the ministry. Increasingly, in the church, the one-man show is out, something I find refreshing and biblical.

But I also find that in our rush to equip laypeople to study the Word, evangelize, teach, and counsel, we often have neglected to train them for one of the most vital areas of ministry: leadership. As important as the usual training is, training for leadership is more so. I agree with Bob Biehl, who said in his *Leadership Wisdom* tape series, "Every organization is a direct reflection of its leadership, for better or worse."

It's no accident that Jesus spent the bulk of his ministry training a small group of future leaders rather than an army of foot soldiers. No doubt he knew the future of the church, humanly speaking, depended upon the quality of its leadership.

Even if there weren't a biblical mandate to equip leaders to lead, the practical benefits would still make it a wise choice.

To begin with, training draws people together. Most church boards are made up of folks from widely divergent backgrounds. But a training program can provide everyone with common experiences and vocabulary, making communication easier.

It doesn't even matter whether everyone agrees with the content of the training. Just going through the process gives us a starting point from which to launch a discussion. It enables us to invest words, terms, and situations with an agreed-upon meaning. That way, even when we disagree, we at least understand one another's frame of reference well enough to intelligently discuss the differences.

Second, training is essential because a church is different from a business organization. It is spiritually centered and run by volunteers. It has a radically different bottom line: relationships. While some of the leadership principles of business carry over, many do not. A training program can help a board to recognize and respond to these differences.

Frankly, it strikes me as ironic that most board members receive so little training today, because the modern-day pastor receives so much. This is the age of continuing education. Additional degrees and further study are not only encouraged; in many cases, they are required. Few churches would settle for a pastor or staff member who lacked formal training.

But if the increasing complexities of ministry necessitate more training for the "professionals," isn't the same needed for the rest of the leadership team? And if as pastor I fail to train leaders to lead, what right do I have to complain about the way board members do their jobs or make their decisions?

As valuable as training can be, if handled poorly, it can do more harm than good. That's why I once wrote an article for LEADERSHIP entitled, "Why Board Training Goes Awry." But if training is done right, it can contribute to a beautiful partnership between pastor and board. Here are some key points I've had to learn.

No lobbying

One of the most important things to remember is the difference between training and lobbying. The two are easily confused.

Training presents information away from the pressure of an immediate decision. *It's designed to change the way we think.*

Lobbying presents information in the middle of the decision-making process. *It's designed to change the way we vote.*

I never fully grasped the difference until we were about to hire our first full-time associate. I had someone in mind, a member of the church who I knew would hit the ground running. I also knew that every church-growth expert agreed we should hire immediately, before the need became acute. That way we would be staffing for growth, not maintenance.

I figured it was an ideal time to teach the board the importance of staffing for growth and the advantages of hiring from within. So I put together a packet of all the literature I could find on the subject, sent it out, and asked everyone to be prepared to discuss it at our next meeting.

When we began our discussion, Jim spoke first. "Thanks for the helpful articles, Larry," he said. "But I know there is always another side to every issue. All these articles agree with you. I'd like to see some from the other side as well."

When I told him there weren't any, that all the experts agreed with me, he looked at me in disbelief. He thought I was lying. It took a long time to convince him otherwise.

I learned a valuable lesson that night. When information is presented in the middle of a decision-making process, most people will look on it as a lobbying effort, not training. Regardless how accurate or helpful the information might be, if it is presented too close to a vote, it will be treated with skepticism—an appropriate response to a lobbyist's presentation.

Yet many of us share the bulk of our insights when an issue is at hand. Until then, the principles we've gleaned from reading, conferences, and experience stay stored in our memory, notebooks, and files. When the board is faced with a tough decision, we pull them out and present them in an attempt to sway their decision. But by then, it is too late. What could have been helpful training comes across as nothing more than manipulative lobbying.

There is another important difference between lobbying and training. *Training* allows people the *freedom and time to change their mind*. *Lobbying* asks for a decision *right now*.

Most of us have had the experience of later championing an

idea we initially rejected. But the change seldom occurs over-night. We need time to reflect and mull over an issue. When I tried to train our board members in the middle of the decision-making process, they had no time to reflect and change their mind. The pressure was on. But now, if they do their best think-ing in the shower or on the way home, that's fine. They have the time to do so.

When John, one of our board members, was first exposed to the principles of church growth, he rejected them *a priori.* "Frankly, this stuff disturbs me," he said at the beginning of one meeting. "We're supposed to be a church, not a business. All these guys care about is numbers."

But with the passage of time and further exposure, he worked through his initial concerns. Now John is one of our board's strongest advocates for growth. More than once he's pointed out an area where we were veering from a basic church-growth principle.

But if John's first exposure to these principles had been dur-ing a major growth-related decision, he would probably still be an opponent. Lobbying would have forced him to digest the information quickly and make a decision. As part of the debat-ing and decision-making process, he would have had to defend his position publicly. And unfortunately, once a person takes a public stand, he seldom changes his mind. It's too threatening to the ego.

Avoiding lobbying removes skepticism and allows people to buy into ideas based on their merit, not our pressure.

Flexibility

Another key to an effective training program is flexibility. For me, that means not being slavishly tied to a set curriculum.

Whenever I talk or write about training leaders, people ask me for a copy of the curriculum we use. They're always sur-prised when I say we have none. Rather than using a set body of material, I select topics of study as we go along, trying to match our training to forthcoming needs.

I realize a curriculum can save time, cover a subject in depth, and add a sense of authority to the things I'm trying to get across.

But once we've started a program, most of us want to stick to it. We then resist excursions down a side road. Yet taking a side road is exactly what I want the freedom to do. I want to deal with issues that soon will be hot and take advantage of teachable moments. Not that I wait until we're in the middle of making a decision (as we've seen, that would be lobbying, not training), but I tackle an issue the moment I see it looming on the horizon.

Say, for example, it's becoming obvious that our growth is going to make an additional service necessary within the next year. I want to be able to stop and study what other churches have done in that situation. And I want us to learn that *now*, well before we're forced to make our own decision.

A second reason why I haven't tried to develop a set curriculum is that I want to stress training as an ongoing process, not a one-time event. Most of us view a training course as something to be finished; once we've completed the material, we consider ourselves trained. That's the last thing I want our leadership team to think. We can't afford to stop learning and growing. To emphasize this, I've chosen to avoid a curriculum with a clearly defined start and end.

In short, it's not easy to be a church leader. The demands on our board constantly change, and new and unforeseen situations crop up. A flexible training program is the only way I can guarantee the board's training will relate to its task.

For instance, a few months ago we had to deal with a case of sexual immorality. What made it difficult was that the sinning brother acknowledged the sin, verbally repented, and put himself into an accountability relationship. But he continued to sin.

We'd never before had a situation in which someone repented and denounced a relationship, and at the same time fell back into it. As a board, we had to make a tough decision. Should we apply the discipline procedures found in 1 Corinthians 5, or keep trying to help this person turn around?

We stopped our current training topic and spent the next couple of sessions wrestling with church discipline, sexual purity, and corporate responsibility. Our study led us to a consensus that as church leaders we could judge people only by their ongoing actions, not their tears, so we asked him to leave the fellowship, which he angrily did. It was a classic teachable moment. I have no doubt that the Bible studies and lessons in that setting never will be forgotten. By keeping ourselves flexible, we were able to study what we needed to know when we needed to know it.

Repetition

Most training programs cover an item once and go on. We tend to think if we have carefully covered an issue once, everyone understands. We forget our own need to hear an idea several times before it soaks in. Also, we fear boring people, so we may move on long before the lesson has been learned.

To keep from doing that, I keep in mind the three stages of learning: exposure, familiarity, and understanding. A lesson hasn't been learned until we've completed the third stage.

The *exposure* stage is by far the most exciting. It's fun to be exposed to new ideas, to wrestle with concepts and principles for the first time. When suddenly I grasp what was only a mystery before, there is a sense of exhilaration.

During the second stage, *familiarity*, there are few surprises. I know where the discussion is going, so there is a great temptation to tune out because "I know this stuff already."

But actually, I don't.

Familiarity falls far short of the final stage of learning: *understanding*. When I'm *familiar* with a subject, I recognize where the teacher is going. When I *understand* a subject, I can teach and apply it myself. Only then has the lesson been learned.

Keeping these three stages in mind has helped me avoid the temptation to move on from an idea too early. For instance, we studied the principles of church growth on and off for about three years. If I had stopped after the first book or a couple of articles, we all would have had a nodding acquaintance with the subject. But we would not have been able to explain church growth to others in the congregation or base decisions on a mature understanding of it.

Even when we fully grasp a subject, it needs to be repeated within a couple of years. Otherwise, a turnover of even a few people can destroy the unified understanding of the board.

Obviously, going over the same material year after year could be a pain for those who have been on the board a long time. To save them the agony, we've put together a starter packet for new board members. It covers material we feel every member needs in order to understand our present board's organizational climate and way of thinking. Our current packet includes four books:

Looking in the Mirror by Lyle Schaller;
The Multiple Staff and the Larger Church, also by Schaller;
Your Church Can Grow by C. Peter Wagner; and
Unleashing the Church by Frank Tillapaugh.

It also includes some articles I've written on the church. With the packet, new board members get a running start, and the gains of today aren't lost tomorrow.

Building Leaders

I once thought equipping the saints for ministry was limited to helping people develop godly character, a knowledge of the Bible, and a specific ministry skill. I left the job of equipping church leaders to the seminaries and Bible schools.

Now, for the sake of our church's long-range health, I've made equipping our leaders to lead a top priority. It has paid off in a board that consistently works through tough issues without losing its cool or its unity.

But the church as a whole has not been the only beneficiary. Our board members have benefited as well. The same principles that made them better church leaders have also helped them lead at home and in the marketplace.

I remember when one elder called to tell me about a major promotion. He was moving into a management position and was going to be overseeing some significant projects. After I congratulated him, he said, "This is a new track for me, but I am excited about it. I've already seen a lot of areas where I can apply the things we've been learning about leadership. I'm confident I'll do a good job."

And he has. His company would be surprised to learn that part of the credit goes to the training he received as an elder in his church.

10

Finding the Fit

Life experiences can open doors to dynamic ministry.

—Ron Oertli

During college, I took a physical education course in boxing. The instructor matched each student with someone of approximately the same height, weight, and reach. But my assigned partner kept missing class, so I frequently ended up boxing a fellow twenty pounds heavier. (I had loose teeth the whole quarter!)

Three one-minute rounds seemed to take forever, especially when the opponent danced around the ring and I connected only once every several punches. Fatigue set in quickly.

I learned a lesson that quarter that has stuck with me ever since: *You're drained of more energy by swinging and missing than by landing a solid punch.*

Now that I am in church ministry, I see a number of people who are worn out in their ministries while others put in a lot more time yet remain refreshed. I suspect that the differences rest not in their commitment level or energy level as much as how well their ministry job fits. When expended energies "connect," people last longer.

You may have heard comments similar to those I sometimes hear: "I'm not sure I belong here anymore. I've been involved in different things, but I don't feel like I fit anywhere. Maybe I should move on."

This kind of comment makes any pastor feel like the spouse who returns home to discover his or her mate has left, leaving a note on the table saying, "We just don't seem meant for each other anymore."

Or perhaps a newcomer to the congregation confesses: "I want to do something, but I'm not sure what I have to offer."

These comments are common in ministry. I recognize them as expressions of a basic Christian need: to be useful and to find a ministry niche.

The church's traditional pattern of fitting available people into existing ministry job slots doesn't usually meet this need. Nor have I found spiritual gifts classes, growth institutes, or seminars particularly helpful. Instead, people received a mish-mash of often excellent material, but a muddle of messages and no clear direction for where to go next.

In 1986, one of our pastors, Tim Robertson, pioneered spiritual planning at Bear Valley Baptist Church. Over a two-year period, he took more than two hundred men and women through spiritual planning and hammered out many of the concepts and methods we still use. Before I took over the responsibility for spiritual planning, I participated as one of the six members of Tim's "think tank." Over the months we brainstormed, dreamed, and worked together to define strategies more clearly.

We worked from two assumptions: (1) God has entrusted to each believer the necessary resources to do what he has called that person to, and (2) God has given each church the people necessary to do what he has called that church to do.

We brainstormed about how to discover the untapped resources already within our congregation. We looked for ways to draw out of individuals how God had especially prepared them for ministry.

We have used three analogies to help clarify what a spiritual planner does. He or she is like:

1. *A financial planner*, who helps people take inventory of resources in order to maximize their financial effectiveness.

2. *A human resource manager*, who helps people select appropriate training and get into the right job.

3. *A career guidance counselor*, who helps people develop a strategy for personal growth and pursue a suitable career.

Three phases make up the spiritual planning process.

First, we ask people to take an inventory of the resources God has entrusted to them (such as spiritual gifts, natural talents, and acquired skills).

Then, based on the church's needs and available opportunities, we propose possible ministries they might pursue.

Finally, we help the individual write a specific plan of action for the next twelve months. This plan includes measurable, attainable goals for growth and ministry as well as a system of accountability.

No doubt other churches might do it differently, but here's what these steps look like for us.

Taking Inventory

Karen had been a Christian for several years but not serious about her faith. One day, she explained, "I'm not sure I have anything to offer the church. I have no idea what special gifts or talents I have. In fact, I'm not sure God even gave me any."

Rather than immediately finding Karen a program to work in, we decided to help her discover the spiritual resources God had provided her. We found that she had organizational and verbal skills. Also, Karen had given birth to a child before she was married and was feeling useless to Christ as a result. We pointed out to her that God could change this difficult life experience into a positive resource. Karen soon became an effective participant in a ministry to young women. So life experiences can open doors to dynamic ministry.

Spiritual gifts also play a role. Helen has a master's degree in education and an excellent reputation in public school classroom teaching, but she has never done well as a Sunday school teacher. During spiritual planning, she concluded that she has the gift of administration. She now helps manage a ministry for women.

We've found that one's secular expertise may not coincide with one's spiritual gift. Scott, an executive-level administrator in a large corporation, has never felt comfortable managing people and activities in the context of ministry. During spiritual planning he decided that, instead, he has the gifts of mercy and teaching. He now works with a support group where people are coming out of difficult life experiences. In addition, he teaches in that context.

We also inquire about what people feel God is calling them to do. People frequently have God-cultivated concerns about particular needs. A certain need may intrigue them or keep them awake at night. We ask individuals if they can identify this type of recurring concern. Stan had a burden for the inner city and now teaches at Denver Street School, helping street people complete their high school education. Dennis serves on the board of the Inner City Health Clinic, but during spiritual planning he recognized his recurring burden for evangelistic outreach to businessmen like himself. He continues as an effective member of the clinic board but has increased his involvement with business contacts.

We call the various ingredients of experience, talents, skills, gifts, education, and burden the "resource mix." People express excitement as they discover strengths they can use more purposefully.

Brian Hathaway, a pastor of the Atatu Bible Chapel in New Zealand, once observed that King David used his natural talent (music) to soothe a troubled king, his acquired skill (with a sling) to slay a ferocious enemy, and his spiritual gift (leadership) to produce a triumphant period in Israel's history. Likewise, we believe God provides each person a unique resource mix.

At Bear Valley, people attend four sessions with one of our trained spiritual planners. The first three sessions focus on the resource mix. Before the first session, we give each person a questionnaire. It must be completed prior to the first session and covers a number of key areas.

The questionnaire also screens out the merely semi-interested people because it requires considerable thought to complete. After looking it over, some people cancel their first appointment. On the other hand, those ready to serve find the questionnaire stimulating.

The Survey

The ten items on the questionnaire explore personal background and interests from several angles. We strongly encourage people to write their answers, although they can simply think through the questions and come prepared to discuss their answers.

1. *Describe your personal, spiritual pilgrimage.* What led to your conversion to Christ? What formal and informal training has contributed to your growth? What crises have you weathered? What have been your experiences in ministry? What individuals have influenced you significantly?

2. *Is God "cultivating a concern" in you for ministry?* What specific needs, issues, or situations particularly touch your heart? What concerns make you want to roll up your sleeves and go to work?

3. *Up to now, what concrete steps have you taken to address these needs or get involved in these issues?*

4. *What do you believe is the general purpose of this spiritual-planning process?*

5. *Specifically identify several things you expect to accomplish through this process.*

6. *Set aside these expectations for the moment and dream.* Assume you had all the resources you wanted and needed, and that God would guarantee your success in anything you wanted to do. Describe what your life would look like ten years from now. Who would you be? What would you be doing?

7. *Identify several resources God has entrusted to you* (spir-

itual gifts, natural talents, acquired skills, experiences).

8. *What is your greatest strength?*

9. *Are there any present barriers keeping you from living up to your God-given potential?* If so, identify them.

10. *Where do you need to grow the most?*

The Sessions

During the first spiritual-planning session, we go over the answers to the questionnaire. We ask permission to take notes and then move through the questions. We ask people to clarify or expand answers we don't fully understand.

Then, typically, the leader will ask people if the process, so far, is meeting their needs. We give them an opportunity to drop out at this point if they wish. But we encourage each person to continue, and we promise to work with those who do. We remind them of the exciting discoveries that lie ahead.

By giving people permission to back out, we provide a graceful exit to those who are not yet ready. We also increase the commitment of those who stay. By the fourth session, those who remain will nearly always be open and ready to be involved in ministry.

At the end of session one, we hand out the Myers-Briggs Type Indicator, explaining that it will give insight into their personality. We hand them a question booklet, an answer sheet, and an envelope with postage on it. People complete the MBTI and mail it back before the second session.

In session two we discuss the results of the MBTI and explain the implications. This exercise helps reveal basic personal preferences. Myers-Briggs functions as a *descriptive* rather than a *prescriptive* tool. It tells how people tend to like to operate in life. A person falls into one of sixteen personality types. Each personality type is identified by four letters. For example, I come out ENTJ.

The EI scale (extroversion/introversion) shows whether an individual focuses attention more on the outer world of people and things or on their inner world of thoughts and understanding.

The SN scale (sensing/intuition) indicates how a person acquires information: empirically through the senses or by intuition.

The TF scale (thinking/feeling) reveals how people make decisions: through objective reasoning or based on personal values.

The JP scale (judging/perceiving) shows the kind of lifestyle a person tends to prefer: orderly and controlled or open-ended and spontaneous.

Often, people find the MBTI segment the most helpful part of all four sessions.

At the end of session two, we provide information on spiritual gifts based on Romans 12, 1 Corinthians 12, Ephesians 4, and 1 Peter 4. People have two weeks to work through the spiritual gifts exercises we assign. They talk to other Christians who know them. They think through what things they have enjoyed doing or have done well. All these activities move them closer to identifying their spiritual gifts.

During the third session we discuss the homework they have done on spiritual gifts. Our experience indicates that most people have more than one spiritual gift—often three or four. We call this their "gift mix." At the end of our third session, we provide printed descriptions of all Bear Valley ministries. In addition, we encourage people to imagine ministries they might like to be involved in that do not yet exist.

Participants leave session three with two assignments. First, based on what they have learned, they pick three or four ministries they might try. Second, they prepare a written action plan.

Development Blueprint

The action plan is a specific, written blueprint for spiritual growth and ministry. It lists goals for the next twelve months in

seven areas: worship, instruction, fellowship, ministry, stewardship, family and friends, and personal development. We discuss the action plan at session four.

Action plans reflect individual differences. One artistic
woman presented her written plan in the form of a beautiful
collage, while an engineer came in with a four-page comput-
erized printout. I recall one person who scribbled out an action
plan on a paper napkin.

Whatever the form, we help people list attainable and measurable goals. Here are examples of the types of goals people
set.

Worship

This includes both corporate and personal worship. One
person may plan to attend Sunday worship more regularly even
when traveling on business or on vacation. Several decided to
have personal devotions ten to fifteen minutes a day, five days
a week. Again, we are not looking for extravagant goals but
ones that are simple and attainable.

Instruction

This may include participation in a Sunday school class and/
or small-group Bible study. A person may commit to reading
two books a month. Another may decide to listen to tapes featuring a Christian speaker. One young man chose to attend a
seminar on leading small groups, a skill he wanted to nurture.

Fellowship

A Sunday school class or Bible study group may provide fellowship as well as instruction. A church softball league may also
suffice. Believers need one another and sometimes must deliberately schedule time for fellowship with others.

Ministry

After people have chosen three or four ministry options
from our opportunity list, they choose one in which they will
likely participate. We want them to be specific: when and where

they'll get involved. We encourage people to try a particular ministry for enough time—generally at least six weeks—to see if the fit is right.

We also encourage each person for the next twelve months to cultivate, with God's help, a close personal relationship with an unbeliever and then, in the context of this friendship, to share the gospel clearly. We want them to experience the adventure and rewards of personal evangelism.

Stewardship

This includes the use of both money and time. Most who come to us want to tithe. We sometimes discover that people are deeply in debt, which has strapped their giving. We then recommend they immediately pursue help from a financial counselor.

We also ask people to be good stewards of their time. One person's goal involved cutting down the amount of overtime he worked to give more time to ministry.

Others feel called to cut back church involvement for the sake of family. Ken was miraculously converted out of a drug culture. He was so excited about his faith that he jumped from one ministry group to another, and he wasn't staying with one thing long enough to truly benefit. In addition, he was not spending enough time at home. During spiritual planning Ken said, "I need some fine tuning. What do you think?" Because of the spiritual planning process, one of our pastors (Ken's spiritual planner) was free to say, "You need to withdraw from your small-group Bible study. You are getting plenty of instruction in your classes at the seminary. Regular time with your wife is more important right now."

Balancing family, career, church, and community remains difficult. At times we simply encourage a commitment to ongoing evaluation. The person may commit, for instance, to sit down each month with his family to discuss their schedules.

Family and friends

We ask each person to list particular goals in regard to their family and friends. Some couples decide to have a date one night each week. One man felt compelled to travel to see both of his adult sons. He hadn't been a Christian when they lived at home. He wanted them to see his new life-style and hear the gospel.

One single woman who earnestly wanted to be married decided to change her hairstyle and to lose weight. She wanted to look as attractive as God made her to be.

Personal development

These goals thrust people beyond their old horizons and boundaries. Their goals may be fun or serious. One man decided to take banjo lessons. Another is now in the process of climbing a number of Colorado's 14,000-foot mountain peaks. A housewife is attending typing classes. Another is learning to play the flute. Several people have pursued fitness goals. These adventures can make a person more capable and more refreshing to be around.

Workable Accountability

The action plan works, of course, only if effective accountability is built into the process. We learned *not* to have pastoral staff and spiritual planners be the ones maintaining accountability. Why? On Sunday some folks scooted around corners when they saw us. Despite our efforts not to make accountability a guilt inducer, they felt guilty and avoided us.

So instead, we have built an accountability system between peers of the same gender. A couple might choose another couple, but usually the wife and husband each choose a separate individual. In any case, each person asks a peer or mentor to serve as an "accountability partner" for a minimum of four meetings during the following twelve months.

The first accountability meeting takes place in thirty days, the second sixty days later. The remaining accountability meetings are quarterly. The church office mails out a gentle reminder before each of the accountability meetings and encloses a postcard to be returned after each meeting.

The accountability people act as mirrors, not judges. They review progress on the action plan. They help people look objectively at their goals and analyze how well they are fulfilling them. If an individual is not meeting her goals, the accountability persons simply ask, "Why?" They do not criticize; they discuss reasons. They suggest possibilities: "Do you think you should redefine your goal?" or "Do you think this goal stretches you enough?"

Does It Work?

As spiritual planning succeeds, we see (1) people living more dedicated and distinctively Christian life-styles and (2) people enjoying effective ministry involvement.

Beth illustrates how this happens.

Beth's ministry experience revolved around Christian education. She had taken seminary courses and taught Sunday school classes. But this ministry gave her little fulfillment. In session one I learned that she had computer expertise; she could write programs in four languages. In addition, she was concerned about, among other things, people withdrawing from cults.

Bear Valley has a ministry called Shield of Faith, which targets people coming out of cults and aberrant Christian groups. And at the time, Shield of Faith desperately needed someone to work with their computers. It was a perfect match! During the spiritual-planning process, Beth was also helped with her devotional life. Later, when Beth's career led her to another city, she wrote us that the spiritual-planning process was one of her most beneficial experiences in Denver.

Many people, of course, are involved in Sunday school classes and other normal church activities when they begin the planning process. And many don't change their ministry involvements. But afterward, they are engaged with greater purpose. Many say, "Now I know why I am doing what I am doing."

And that not only strengthens them, but it solidifies the church, which, as Paul observed, "grows and builds itself up in love, as each part does its work" (Ephesians 4:16).

11

The Care and Feeding of Leaders

*I learned the hard way that church leaders need
personalized care.*

—Roy C. Price

I 've just gone through one of the most painful periods in my
pastoral experience. It revolved around my relationship with
one man. From the first time I met him, things were strained. A
former leader in our church, he lived in another state for a few
years and then returned to his position on the board. In the interim, I had come to the church as pastor.

Early on I sensed negative vibrations from this person.
About the same time I began to initiate monthly luncheons with
each board member, but he wouldn't meet with me. The end
result was that he left the church. Although I leave the matter
with God, I'm convinced that had I begun meeting individually
with my board earlier, it would have made a difference. I
learned the hard way that church leaders need personalized
care.

The Power of Personal Influence

"It's so simple! Why didn't I do this before?" I exclaimed to
my wife after having lunch with one of my board members. The
need for better communication with the board had been apparent, but I hadn't been sure how to go about it.

After considering several options, I had decided to begin having regular luncheons or breakfasts with them individually. No agenda. No pressure. We talked about their areas of responsibility and prayed together. I came away knowing my leaders better, sensing their concerns about the church and about their own lives.

About the same time I read a comment by Richard Halverson: "Whether a pastor is starting a new church or beginning his ministry in an established one, he will find Jesus' fundamental strategy of personally training individual leaders to be the key for a strong, healthy church with an effective outreach."

That made sense to me. In a way, I had always believed it, but I had allowed this productive idea to get squeezed out of my calendar. I rationalized that the leaders were too busy with their jobs and families to spend time with me. But the truth was, I was allowing myself to be swamped with the immediate and had lost my priorities.

Not long ago I had a chance to ask Dr. Halverson a question: "What do you do when you can't get along with a board member?"

"I had such a man on my board once," he recalled. "He was very strong, with definite convictions about everything. He had the kind of wisdom that comes more from experience than from education. We clashed.

"But after many struggles, we came to have a very close relationship. I could go confidently to him and get the support I needed.

"How did this happen? I've learned through the years that struggle deepens intimacy. The approach I've used when having difficulty with a brother is to love him, submit to him, and pray much."

Donald Bubna, pastor-at-large for the Christian and Missionary Alliance denomination, tells of a persistently strained relationship with a church leader that began shortly after he arrived at a church in the early '60s. "We had radically different personalities. It strained our relationship. Yet over the years, through mutual discipling and praying together, we've become very special brothers."

How was this change possible? Pastors have two sources of power: their position and their personal influence. In position power, a job gets done by someone in the church because the *pastor* asked him or her to do it. The person might grumble and fuss during the project, but he feels the intimidating power of pastoral authority driving him to do the work.

What is the power of personal influence? Paul Hershey and Kenneth Blanchard, in their book *Management of Organizational Behavior*, describe it this way: "To the extent that followers respect, feel good about, and are committed to their leader, they will see their goals satisfied through the goals of their leader." When there is internal motivation, close supervision is not required, and the leader is effective. This is the kind of leadership that makes pastors effective in their work. It also reduces tension and stress.

Unfortunately, we pastors can tend to be more concerned about tasks than people. We have sermons to prepare, committees to attend, agendas to develop, hospital calls to make, bulletins and orders of service to write. We communicate a lack of trust when we refuse to delegate tasks and then give people the freedom to pursue the task in their own style. By encumbering ourselves with paper shuffling, we lose contact with people.

The cure to this is spending more time with key leaders. Make no mistake, this will take time and some rearrangement of your ordinary schedule. But more than that, it will require an adjustment in your thinking. Here are two ways to care for and feed your leaders.

Commit to leadership development

I'd like to suggest four reasons why this makes sense:

1. *It deepens personal relationships.*

The quality of interpersonal relationships with layleaders will spell success or defeat for a pastor. In most churches, it's impossible to know everyone intimately, but it is possible with a select group of leaders. This means spending personal time with them. Mark 3:14 (NASB) tells us Jesus "appointed twelve, that they might be with Him." By the time the apostles were on their own, they had gained the reputation of being "little Christs." How did they get that way? By being with Jesus.

2. It deepens spiritual relationships.

In making a disciple, I teach him to obey the words of Jesus. God told Joshua that the key to his success would be obedience to the Word. It hasn't changed through the centuries. My effectiveness with my leadership is directly proportional to my helping them grow in their understanding of the Bible.

Realizing this a few years ago, I asked a group of men to meet me for Scripture memory and prayer while we had breakfast. They thought that was a great idea and selected six o'clock Monday morning! More mornings than not, I had to force the covers back at five o'clock, slide out of bed, and dash cold water on my face in order to make it to breakfast only half asleep. But I so needed that fellowship that I stayed with it. And although I left the church five years ago, that little group still meets every week.

3. It equips for ministry.

Halverson had a superb approach to new ideas or program innovations: "Rarely do I put myself in the position of having someone oppose my proposals. If I have what I believe is a good idea, I plant it in the mind and heart of someone else and allow it to grow there. I do this by asking them what they think about it and to pray about it, without putting them under any pressure to approve it or support it. I think of ideas as seeds rather than bullets. I plant them rather than hit people with them. It takes longer this way, but the long-term results are far superior."

Donald Bubna seeks to equip his leadership through the sub-parish system. His church has a total of twelve groups under the direction of elders. The elders are in turn divided into three groups, with one staff member assigned to each. Don has done inductive Bible studies with these men and other potential leaders to develop their research and study skills. The classes require three to five hours of preparation each week. In this way, the personal ministry filters down to the personal level through lay leadership.

It is worth saying, in a day when discipleship is the hot-selling theme, that *all* ministries of a biblical church are discipling ministries. Preaching, choral work, other musical expressions, all phases of Christian education, women's mission work, service projects, and home Bible studies are all part of discipling. Let's not slip on the banana peel of false guilt simply because we don't have the newer forms of some programs. The church has discipled for 2,000 years, or there wouldn't be a church today.

4. It improves communication.

Good communication builds trust. After Jesus had taught the people, he asked Peter to put out into the lake to catch some fish. The sky was blue with a gentle breeze blowing cotton-like clouds. Peter was tired. All night he had been fishing with no results. He protested, but in condescension to Jesus' wish he lowered the nets. The haul was so great they called for help. Fish flipped everywhere, and the boats were filled to the point of sinking. Their catch that day may have financed several months of ministry. It made a believer out of Peter. This was the turning point of his commitment, for he found Jesus to be greater than his own vocational skills.

A pastor doesn't have to catch the most fish to win the confidence of his leaders, but he does have to be with them. They need to know him as a man in touch with their world. When two men pray, the masks are off, and loving acceptance and trust can be established. The gospel accounts indicate that the Pharisees and other religious leaders were aloof from the people, while Jesus was with them. He understood them, being one of them, and they trusted him. Peter was even willing to fight for Jesus in the garden. Pastors could benefit from that kind of loyalty once in a while.

Choose effective leaders

Although every church has formal leadership (those elected), it also has informal leaders. The pastor needs to determine which leadership will produce the long-term benefits. Two basic questions, for instance, might help identify potential leaders:

1. *Is there a desire to learn or grow?*

Every church board ought to get away at least once a year, preferably with their mates, for spiritual refreshment. A board member must want to do that. It can do much to develop warmth, acceptance, and trust. In addition, I have found it extremely helpful to have regular Saturdays of work or study together on church matters.

2. *Is there a willingness to give priority to time together?*

Discipling demands commitment. You can't instill life in the dead. We need to love and pray for everyone but put our energies into lives that are responsive and eager to grow. A leader who wants to grow will take time to cultivate growth.

Whatever pattern a pastor may adopt, the benefits of spending personal time with lay leadership make it worthwhile: the warmth of knowing your people and their knowing you; the removal of negative filters that distort communication; the personal enrichment of lives; the resolution of conflicts before they become big issues; and the building of trust because staff and laity know there is love for one another.

Although it is axiomatic that the church goes on when the pastor leaves, it is also true that a pastor's effectiveness is measured by the quality of people he leaves behind. If he has spent time with them, they will carry the benefits of that time into the future of the church.

12

Making Ministry Healthy

*It is possible for an unhealthy pastor to lead
a growing church, but it takes a healthy pastor to lead
a healthy church.*

—Rick Warren

I have a problem with the idea of numerical church growth being the primary focus of pastors. In the early 1980s I used the term "church growth" because that was what everybody was familiar with. But I stopped using the phrase around 1986 because of the things I didn't like about the church growth movement.

For one thing, I don't like the incessant comparing of churches. The Bible says it's foolish to compare yourself to others. If you find somebody who's doing a better job than you, you get discouraged. If you find you're doing a better job than someone else, you could become proud. Either way, you're dead in the water.

A far better focal point than growth is health. Size is not the issue. You can be big and healthy, or big and flabby. You can be small and healthy, or small and wimpy. Big isn't better; small isn't better. Healthy is better. So I'm interested in helping churches become balanced and healthy.

If churches are healthy, growth is a natural occurrence. I don't have to command my kids to grow. If I provide them with a healthy environment, growth is automatic. If growth is not happening, it means something's wrong because it's the nature of living organisms to grow. Church growth automatically means numerical growth to most people, but that's only one kind of growth God is looking for in his church.

Putting the focus on church health can raise a problem, though. Attendance is much easier to measure. So how do we know whether a church is healthy?

Health Indicators

Actually, numerical growth is not an unreliable indicator of health; it is merely inadequate. There are five ways to measure growth. A church needs to grow warmer through fellowship, deeper through discipleship, stronger through worship, broader through ministry, and larger through evangelism.

You don't judge an army's strength by how many people sit in the mess hall. You judge an army on the basis of how many people are trained and active on the front line. The percentage of members being mobilized for ministry and missions is a more reliable indicator of health than how many people attend services. A church that's running an average attendance of 200 in a town of a thousand is doing a better job than Saddleback Valley Community Church.

Consider one church I heard about in rural Indiana where their children's program reaches 40 percent of the kids in the school district! That's a highly effective church. Percentage-wise, that beats anything we're doing here. A church may max out its numerical growth potential because of location, but it can continue its effectiveness.

Another mark of maturity is the ability to start having children. I want to see churches that are plateaued in numerical growth begin to reproduce through church planting. We're now in the grandparenting phase; we have churches that were started by churches started by Saddleback. That's a lot of fun because we get the credit but we don't have to mess with the dirty diapers.

Then once we have a sense of what characterizes a healthy church, how do we go about developing it?

Health Cultivation

Health is the result of balance. Balance occurs when you have a strategy and a structure to fulfill what I believe are the five New Testament purposes for the church: worship, evangelism, fellowship, discipleship, and ministry. If you don't have a strategy and a structure that intentionally balances the purposes of the church, the church tends to overemphasize the purpose the pastor feels most passionate about.

In evangelicalism, we tend to go to seed on one truth at a time. You attend one seminar and hear, "The key is seeker services." You go to another and "the key is small groups" or "discipleship" or "expository preaching." The fact is, they're all important. When a church emphasizes any one purpose to the neglect of others, that produces imbalance—it's unhealthy. It stunts a lot of churches.

To keep things balanced, four things must happen. You've got to move people into membership, build them up to maturity, train them for ministry, and send them out on their mission. We use a little baseball diamond to illustrate that. We've got a scorecard to evaluate progress. Just like when you go to a doctor and he checks all your vital signs, the health of a church is quantifiable. For example, I can measure how many more people are involved in ministry this month than last month.

How you accomplish those four objectives doesn't matter. Some will look at the rapid growth in our church and attribute it to Saddleback's unique style of ministry. People always overemphasize style because it's the first thing they notice. The only important issue regarding style is that it matches the people God has called you to reach. We've planted twenty-six daughter churches, and we gave the pastors of those congregations total freedom in matters of worship style and the materials they use. As long as you are bringing people to Christ, into the fellowship of his family, building them up to maturity, training them for ministry, and sending them out in mission, I like the way you are doing ministry.

Health does not mean perfection. When a church focuses on evangelism, it brings in a lot of unhealthy people. My kids are healthy; they're not perfect. There will never be a perfect church this side of heaven because every church is filled with pagans, carnal Christians, and immature believers along with the mature ones.

I've read books that emphasize, "You've got to reinforce the purity of the church." But Jesus said, "Let the tares and the wheat grow together, and one day I'll sort them out." We're not in the sorting business. We're in the harvesting business. We do get a lot of unhealthy people at church because society is getting sicker. But Jesus demonstrated that ministering to hurting people was more important than maintaining purity. When you fish with a big net, you catch all kinds of fish.

That's why one of the biggest programs in our church is recovery. We have five to six hundred people attend Friday night recovery meetings with you-name-it addictions. One of the most important decisions we made was not to have a counseling center. If we put a full-time therapist on our staff, the person's schedule would fill up instantly, and 99 percent of the calls would still go unmet. We couldn't keep up even if we had five full-time therapists. Instead, we've trained about fifty laypeople to do biblical counseling, along with a standard list of approved therapists we can refer to if need be.

First Things First

Growing a healthy church depends on the personal character of the leader. It is possible for an unhealthy pastor to lead a growing church, but it takes a healthy pastor to lead a healthy church. You can't lead people further than you are in your own spiritual health.

Several traits indicate to me that a pastor is healthy.

The first is authenticity. That means you are aware of your weaknesses and publicly admit them. I'm convinced that our greatest ministry to others comes out of our weaknesses, not our strengths. You can impress people from a distance, but you can only influence them up close. And if you're going to influence people, you better be honest, even about your weaknesses.

Last weekend at our men's retreat, for example, I talked about how my wife and I went for sexual therapy. That blew some people away. My wife was molested as a little girl; it caused all kinds of problems in our marriage. I went to therapy thinking she had a problem. But once we got there, I realized I had some attitudes that were perpetuating the problem. I tell those stories so people know that we've got real problems, too.

Related to authenticity is humility. (It's hard to talk about how important it is to be humble. You can't say, "Read my best-selling book on being a humble pastor.") It's no accident that humor and humility come from the same root word. Humility is not denying your strengths; it's being honest about your weaknesses. I've built a staff that makes me look good because they compensate for my weaknesses. I do what I'm competent in, and I don't do what I'm not competent in.

Next is integrity. Is there congruence between what you say is important in your life and what you actually do?

In addition, a healthy pastor is always learning. I read almost a book a day. I read early in the morning and late at night. I've learned to get the ideas of a book quickly, to skim fast. Not every chapter in a book is of value. I flip through magazines everywhere I go. The moment you stop growing, your church stops growing.

I must give up some things in order to continually read and learn, and television is an easy choice. I haven't completely given it up, but you don't have to watch *Seinfield* or *Home Improvement* every week to know exactly what's going on. I flip through *TV Guide* once a week to see if there's anything I need to videotape, and then I'll watch it when it fits into my schedule.

And just as churches need balance, pastors do, too. "Blessed are the balanced, for they shall outlast everybody else." So many pastors flame bright, then flame out.

While most of us would say that balance is important in our personal lives, it usually takes a crisis to get our attention. When we began Saddleback, I was imbalanced. I burned out by the end of the first year, and I was depressed all of the next year. My prayer was not "God, build a great church." It was "God, just let me live through the next week."

But it's good to have your losses right up front. The lessons I learned in that second year of depression saved me from flaming out for good. I set parameters. You've got to know who you are, who you're trying to please, and what contribution God wants you to make.

Some people run themselves ragged by speaking all over the country. I don't speak at national events because there's a crowd. I'm a trainer at heart, and I usually only leave our congregation to train other pastors. I'm a local church pastor, and nothing is more fulfilling to me than pastoring my congregation. I don't really care to be a celebrity on the circuit.

So to be healthy, I have to know my focus, my strengths, and my limitations. One limitation I have, for example, is that I was born with a brain malfunction. I took medicine from the time I was a child until college because I would often faint. I could be sitting in a classroom and just keel over. I even had to take a year off from college because of this. It was a scary time. I've been under the care of the best neurologists around. It's complicated, but a simplistic explanation is that my brain has an unusual reaction to adrenaline. (It's a good thing I have a low-stress job.) When a normal amount of adrenaline hits my system, I get dizzy and can black out. My vision remains blurred, my head throbs, and I feel intense panic until the adrenaline goes down. It's like hanging on to the top of the Empire State Building with one finger and looking down—absolute terror.

Now, anybody who speaks knows adrenaline is the pastor's

best friend. It gives you passion, alertness, and energy. The very thing I need to accomplish what God has called me to do, however, acts like a poison for me. I guess it's a thorn in the flesh. When I speak, I'm often unable to clearly see the congregation during the first several minutes of the normal adrenaline rush. People look blurry, I feel panic, and it is extremely painful to speak. I have asked a team to pray for me the entire service, during each of the four services. People ask me, "Do you ever get full of pride speaking to all those people?" Honestly, that's the last thing on my mind. I'm praying, "God, get me through this. Use this weak vessel, and in my weakness, you be strong."

Another practical skill that helps keep me healthy is learning how to refuel—physically, emotionally, spiritually. For example, I've learned to fall asleep in about five minutes. Last Saturday, I spoke twice at our men's retreat. On the way back, I took a brief nap in the car, and I was able then to speak at two services that night. You can't land every time you're tired. You've got to learn to refuel in midair.

To refuel, I do three things:

- Divert daily—do something that's fun.
- Withdraw weekly—a day off every week.
- Abandon annually—get away from your church to vacation, and don't call in.

I stick with that fairly well and insist on it with my staff, too. It is a law at Saddleback that staff cannot work more than three nights in any week. I think the reason many pastors flame out in moral failure is that fatigue lowers our sensibility. One pastor described his affair by saying, "I was under such stress that I pulled the trigger, then ran around and stood in front of the gun." The only way he could get off the fast track was to sabotage himself.

Refueling is more important than having an accountability group. I think accountability is overrated. It works only if you want it to. If I don't really want you to know the truth, you're not going to know the truth. The guy I just quoted had an accountability group.

A final side of balance, of course, is with my family. I don't think my family's health has been negatively affected by my ministry. My wife and I are pastors' kids, so we knew exactly what we were getting into. The previous generation said, "If you put God first, then God will take care of your kids." We believe that, but that's *not* the same as putting the church first.

So I've tried to demonstrate that my family is more important than our church in practical ways, such as not preaching at a Saturday service in order to take my daughter to a special school function. For years our youngest son didn't want to attend our children's camp. But last summer he said, "Dad, I'll go to camp if you'll go with me." Well, there was no question about it; I was going. But I was scheduled to speak at a preliminary Promise Keepers event for pastors in Atlanta. I canceled speaking at the PK event in order to be with my son.

Health Maintenance

What are my goals for the future?

Well, I'm getting back into blues guitar. It's a great stress reliever for a frustrated rock star like me! (You oughta hear my "Backslider Blues," baby!) If you live in California, you've got to be bilingual, so I'm hoping to learn Spanish. But mostly I just want to keep sharpening the skills I've developed so far, simply doing everything better—communicating, caring, planning, leading.

I have no plans to move out of local church ministry in the second half of life. I'm not going anywhere. I'll pastor Saddleback, and at the same time continue to train pastors in how to grow healthy, balanced, purpose-driven churches.

Last year I was asked to consider becoming CEO of the Southern Baptist's North American Mission Board. It's a mammoth organization with a $100 million budget, but I knew I was not the man. I love being a pastor. One reason pastors listen to me is that they know I'm still changing diapers every week. I'm at bat every six days. I still deal with cantankerous members. Pastoring keeps me honest as a trainer.

I hope that Saddleback can continue to be part of the research and development department of the church at large. We're not afraid to fail. We've always tried more things that didn't work than did. Every once in a while we find—usually by accident—something that works. Then we teach the seminars and pretend that we planned it all along, when really it was only the result of trial and error.

One thing I have learned about staying healthy that I didn't know starting out is that I need to offer my resignation to Christ every Sunday. That causes me to hold God's gift with an open hand, and the stress factor goes way down because my identity is not tied to integers. I've seen pastors toward the end of their ministry who start holding on. They're afraid to let go even when they stay beyond their effectiveness. We've all seen professional athletes who played two seasons too long. It's only when you don't have to stay that you can stay.

13

Turning Committees into Community

*Prior to performers, we're people who have
to care for each other.*

—Roberta Hestenes

We dreaded the meeting but attended once a month anyway. It always ran long. We usually went home frustrated. None of us, if we were honest, could say we *enjoyed* the meetings of our board.

One night the issue was how to revitalize our worship services, which we all agreed were flat. Someone had argued at a previous session that the elders should "exercise some responsibility."

The solution: We organized a committee and assigned an elder to be in charge. What happened? Nothing. Month after month, no report, no report, no report. The tension and pressure kept rising.

Each meeting began to follow a pattern: After prayer we'd go directly into committee reports. Although scheduled, we'd get to old or new business only rarely. We would rehash each committee's report or, in the case of the worship committee, the nonreport.

Bob, the chairman of the board, would make a speech lamenting comments gathered from parishioners who took him into their confidence that month. He'd report that there were "some people" about to leave the church.

Jim, the music director, would respond defensively, saying he had received only positive comments and was still awaiting guidance from the worship committee.

Bill, the worship committee chairman, would invariably have another explanation for why the committee was unable to meet or still wasn't ready to offer recommendations.

Speeches would get louder and less subtle. And all this over how to worship the God of love!

One night, as I pulled into the parking lot, I couldn't help but wonder, *If we leaders of the church don't know how to be the church to one another as we do church business, where will we ever be the church?*

The Other Extreme

Some people react to the distasteful side of working within a church structure by avoiding the institutional responsibilities. Their involvement in church extends no further than worship and home Bible studies or support groups.

Many people attracted to these relational groups want little to do with filling traditional roles in the church. They expect Sunday school and child care during the worship services. They enjoy hearing a choir and quality music. They'll participate in the church programs, but they don't want to get into the structure themselves. That doesn't "meet their needs."

If an institutional functionary talked honestly with one of the relational groupies, the conversation might sound something like this:

Charlie (the institutionalist): I helped found this church and served as its chairman for ten years. I've seen Bible studies and young couples come and go. But the church and its programs continue. Frankly, I'm tired of people coming and talking, enjoying the benefits of the program, and never contributing.

Ron (the relationalist): Committees and bureaucratic offices leave me cold. I want to be in a group that shares needs and relates the Bible to what's going on in the real world. Hasn't the church grown since we've started so many small groups?

Charlie: If the church has grown, why are we struggling to keep its programs afloat? Why aren't we meeting our missions budget? Why the shortage of Sunday school teachers? Why are Sunday evening and midweek services so poorly attended? It seems your relations-ministry people don't really care about the church.

Ron: But don't you see? We *are* the church!

Charlie: Well then, maybe we should start passing the offering plate at these groups to support the missions program. Maybe you should cancel your home Bible study the week we have a revival scheduled. Maybe your people should take responsibility for the church by filling more positions. To be honest, I'm getting burned out from giving and giving and never getting my own needs met.

Ron: But that's what our groups are all about—meeting needs!

Charlie: Then why don't they start meeting some of the church's needs by relieving some of us who shoulder the administrative load for the rest of you?

Expectation Gap

To some extent these different perspectives reflect a generational gap. Often the younger church members (twenties and thirties) are more attracted to the relational approach. They prefer relationships defined more by quality than by formal titles. They come to a church and ask, "How can I use my gifts?" If the answer is "Join a committee," they say, "That isn't what I asked."

Relational people aren't motivated by tradition or denominational loyalty. They want to know, *Will this activity give me a meaningful, authentic, significant experience?* They want to feel they count as individuals. They want their personal concerns recognized. A task-oriented committee usually feels, to them, cold and impersonal.

Program-oriented people, on the other hand, tend to hold an older view that sees talking about yourself and your problems as boorish and impolite. If you have tension in your family, telling people who are not related by blood or marriage violates a basic taboo: *We are loyal within our family; we do not tell outsiders what is wrong with us.* The way to handle a bad day, they feel, is to put on a good face, do what has to be done, and move forward without griping about it. Anything else is bad form.

The relational person reacts: "If we can't talk about real stuff and real life—if I have to sit here and play phony games—I don't have the time, energy, or interest. I'll add another involvement only if the situation enables me to satisfy those needs that go unmet in the world. Everywhere else, I have to pretend I'm competent and in control. I don't want to come to church to pretend."

Institutionalists see themselves not as pretending but as selflessly getting things done. To them, the bottom line for a committee is, what have we accomplished and how much did it cost?

When one group finds fulfillment through relationships and the other through the exercise of power, tension between the two is inevitable. The people trying to keep the institution on course will become increasingly discouraged about not having enough money, resources, or support for what they are doing.

The relational people will build small-group networks and attract people who find these groups meaningful. But as the church begins to grow (and with it, demands on the program), the institutional people will ask why the relational people don't "get with the program."

Mission-Focused Community

A turning point for me came when I asked myself, "How does ministry happen?" I realized I had a whole group of people committed to ministry. They were the people in the structure.

Yet they needed more than they were getting.

They experienced church in two places: in the worship service and on committees. They had an unspoken assumption that in a committee you no longer live under biblical guidelines; you live by Roberts Rules of Order. It was almost as if Jesus said, "Love one another—unless you're in a committee meeting. In that case, love takes a backseat to getting your point across."

Once, while at lunch with an elder, he looked me in the eye and said, "Okay, now tell me what you want."

"What do you mean?" I asked.

"I've never been to lunch with a pastor who didn't want me to do something." It took me the rest of our time together to convince him I only wanted to get acquainted, to find out how his life was going and how I might better pray for him. I had no hidden agenda.

The program-oriented person isn't used to being nourished as a person rather than a producer. But concern for the personal side is necessary to sustain anyone in a ministry. Even institutional people, who work with a deep sense of loyalty, commitment, and duty, will end up getting burned out or cynical if they try to make the church work effectively without receiving personal care.

One sign of this is, whenever I meet elders and board members from other churches, I ask how they'll feel the day their term is up. The overwhelming response is "Relieved! I'm not really satisfied in this. I am doing it because it needs to be done."

This fatally flawed perspective fails to see roles as ministries carried out in the context of community. Unless leaders catch this vision, the church can never be anything more than an institution.

I obviously reject both the impersonal committee approach and the ingrown, feel-good group approach. We need a new understanding of how we minister together. I've called this new approach a "mission-focused community."

What a Mission-Focused Community Is

Committees traditionally fall short of being true mission-focused communities in a number of areas.

Commitment

For the average committee member, commitment means: "I come to meetings and respond to anything I'm supposed to vote on. If something doesn't happen, it isn't my fault; I'm not responsible for taking initiative unless it's on the agenda."

In addition, the traditional time commitment is usually inadequate. Most committees assume a handful of people meeting once a month can renew a church in areas like worship or Christian education or discipleship. What often happens is this: We take a month to recruit people. We don't meet in August or between Thanksgiving and Christmas. The flu wipes out February. By year's end, we've met eight or nine times, usually starting late or with latecomers yet to arrive, and sometimes ending three hours later. On an average night only two hours are actually productive.

Two hours times nine is supposed to revitalize our church in adult education? It wouldn't even provide minimal maintenance. Actually, we have programmed ourselves for nongrowth and noncreativity.

Frequency

A committee usually meets according to a set calendar. A mission-focused community, on the other hand, meets as often as is necessary to get the task done.

In one church the evangelism committee met each month and issued a report on how somebody else should do something about evangelism:

"The pastor should give more invitations."

"The congregation should get out and win neighbors to Christ."

As far as I know, not a single person came to church or accepted Christ as a result of that committee, but it met faithfully and cranked out resolutions.

Finally, a new chairman announced he would quit unless the committee took the lead and became active in evangelism personally. The group accepted the challenge and became a mission community. Sometimes they met for a whole day at a time. Sometimes months passed without a meeting because the group had no need to meet, but they always kept in touch. Each person grasped what needed to be done and did it. By the end of the year, more than one hundred people had professed Christ as a direct outcome of that committee's ministry.

Calling

"Please tell people," my banker friend pleaded, "that bankers don't necessarily want to serve on the finance committee." One accountant friend says, "I keep ending up as finance committee chairman, but that's what I do all day! I really want to work with kids, but nobody asks me because they assume my life's vocation indicates my church calling. Well, it just ain't so."

In the traditional system, a nominating committee would have put Saul, the tentmaker from Tarsus, on the maintenance committee. Men like Saul will cheerfully do this work, but they need a way to discover other gifts.

Calling also influences the number and type of groups formed. In many churches, certain committees exist because they have always existed, whether currently needed or not, and needs may exist for which there are no committees. Mission communities, on the other hand, form in response to real needs and are staffed by people who have chosen that mission personally and whose gifts and calling determine their roles.

A prison ministry group, for instance, may form because some people feel called to that ministry. Other mission communities may develop that other churches in the denomination don't have, but they uniquely fit this congregation's situation and the people's need and sense of call.

For roles to be self-chosen, you may have to set needs and

tasks before your people and ask, "Which do you feel called and committed to doing?" In one church I worked in for over ten years, we found people became more committed to their ministries when we gave them time to pray, talk about the needs, and choose their tasks themselves. They now owned the problem and the solution; they didn't grudgingly accept an assignment. Energy levels rose because it was no longer "this is a job someone else stuck me with."

Responsibility

In one church, a four-person elder board didn't like how the Christian education office looked. They reasoned, "We are elders; we have the authority." So one Saturday they came in and rearranged it. When the women who ran the program—recruiting teachers, ordering supplies, and arranging the lessons—came in on Sunday, they were confused and dismayed. They quit on the spot.

Traditional committees often separate authority from responsibility, and this is deadly. Committee members end up with a low sense of responsibility for their decisions, while those who do the work often lack authority needed to make responsible decisions.

Mission-focused communities, on the other hand, tend to keep responsibility and authority closer together.

Uninvited guests

There are always *invited* guests at a conventional committee meeting: our brains and our seats. We are supposed to bring ideas and information and sit as long as the meeting runs.

The *uninvited* guests are our emotions, family problems, and personal concerns. Like little gremlins, they sneak in and mess up a meeting by discharging frustrations in speeches on topics totally unrelated to what is really bothering us.

When you hear anger in someone's voice, probably this person is tired or stressed out or somebody didn't treat her right. She has all these feelings, but because feelings weren't invited to the party she can't deal with them directly.

This harms more than the effectiveness of the committee. It fails the individual who came to a group of believers, where help should be available.

One way of identifying all the guests is to have everyone answer a brief question—either for the whole group or in smaller groups of three or four. Some people feel uncomfortable with anything too personal. But if they feel the discussion is relevant to the ministry assignment, they'll share. For instance, if we're to discuss an evangelism report, I might ask, "What most influenced you to come to Christ?" Or before discussing worship, "What was your most meaningful worship experience?" The key is to ask questions related to the assignment while avoiding loaded questions and ones some cannot answer.

In a community, there are no uninvited guests. The whole person is invited. We take time to catch up with one another, pray for needs, and *then* go on to business. Before we do business, we need to know who is here—physically and emotionally—and what we have to work with.

Getting There

I began this chapter with our governing board's dilemma— a worship committee that wasn't reporting. The episode turned out nothing like I would have imagined. In fact, the actual events proved to be a major step toward community for our leaders and the church.

As it happened, we decided to spend the first fifteen minutes in groups of four or five to discuss three questions:

1. What has your week been like?
2. How can we pray for you?
3. What is one area of your ministry we can pray for?

I ended up in the group with the worship committee chairman, who shared last: "Well, this week's been like all my others. You know my wife is dying of cancer." (We knew nothing of the sort!)

"I get home from work and cook the meals. I put the kids and Irene to bed, and it's midnight. Then I drop into bed to do it all again seven hours later. As for ministry, I just can't seem to get anything accomplished. Taking care of Irene takes every bit of energy I have. I wish you would pray for me."

At that point all our ill feelings toward this man dissolved. Instead of being irritated, we were devastated. Not one of us had prayed for him during these months. We criticized him. We gossiped about him and wondered why he didn't get off the dime.

"Why didn't you tell us sooner?" I asked.

"Somehow it never seemed appropriate," he said. "What was I to do, interrupt a discussion of the music director's ideas to say, 'By the way, things are bad at home'? Besides, I was afraid I might cry."

I resolved at that point never again to let committee business squeeze out the community essential to being the church. It doesn't matter what problem or project we're working on: prior to performers, we're people who have to care for each other. And that makes us work together even more effectively.

14

How to Lead and Feed

*I want to be the warm and gentle pastor who comforts
and the visionary leader who challenges.*

—Jack Hayford

One Saturday years ago some stunning, painful news came
to me. Through a counseling conversation, I discovered
that a pastor in our church had fallen into adultery. Since I
trusted the person giving me this information, I knew I had to
act—but what should I do exactly? I didn't want to presume his
guilt; then again, if he was at fault, I had to deal with him.

The following Tuesday, that same pastor snapped at another
staff member, so I decided to call him into my office to talk
about that. Meanwhile, I hoped he would acknowledge his immorality in the course of the conversation.

Having known and even been involved in the training of this
young man for years, I could be direct. In fact, I was pretty hard
on him about his snapping remark. "We don't treat each other
like that," I stressed. Then, spontaneously, I added, "But that's
not the only problem here, is it?"

He looked up at me, began to tremble, hung his head, and
wept.

I wept with him. He was not an evil man, but he had succumbed to weakness.

In the days that followed, I walked a fine line. I needed to
lead, to take a strong stand against sexual sin, both with this

man in private and before the entire church. Yet I needed to be pastoral, bringing healing and restoration. Both were essential for this individual and his wife as well as the church.

This is just one example of the tension between leading and feeding. And it *is* a tension.

When a pastor primarily feeds, people enjoy the church but lack a corporate sense of destiny. They graze comfortably in the valley and never climb to new heights. The church has a warm, fuzzy feeling, and people enjoy the inspiration and fellowship, but they're not trying to achieve anything. Sheep don't want to climb mountains. They're happy as long as they have a patch of grass.

If a pastor emphasizes leading, on the other hand, he or she may drive the sheep into the ground, pushing them up the mountain without allowing them to stop and eat. If the flock makes it to the top, they're dizzy with weariness, and the burn-out quotient increases.

I want to be the warm and gentle pastor who comforts *and* the visionary leader who challenges. I've found, although difficult at times, it's possible to do both.

The Difficulties

In some ways, leading and feeding can complement each other. But we should be aware of the special problems and difficulties that arise as we try to do both. Here are a few issues that challenge me.

1. *Difficult people.*

Some people are parasites. Often something terrible happened in their past, and no matter how much attention you give them, they want more, personally, from you alone. When they touch you, you can feel the energy drain right out of you.

In dealing with such people, I am torn between caring for them and attending to the leadership tasks that benefit the entire church. I seek to show warmth and acceptance, while others with a gift for merciful ministry give greater, sustained attention to those needy, draining types.

As these individuals call the weaker person to Christian growth and discipline, I buttress their demands and declared expectations. So I'm more than just "a nice guy." My acceptance lays a foundation for the effective ministry of mercy by others—and the tension between leading (calling to growth) and feeding (patient nurturing) is maintained.

2. Misunderstandings.

When dealing with issues such as personal evangelism, faith promises for missions, tithing, or personal devotions, I cringe at the misconceptions people have. Many of their false assumptions can too easily cause misunderstandings. For instance, in each of our church services, we have twenty to forty visitors who, when I talk about money, could immediately assume, *That's what I thought. They're after my money.*

So I'll often begin a discussion of money with a few qualifiers. "If you're attending our church for the first time, you need to know that I do not preach about money every week. It is an important subject for every Christian, and Jesus emphasized the impact that money has on our spiritual lives, but it is not the primary subject of the Bible or of my preaching. It just so happens that I'm talking about it today. My goal in preaching about money is to strengthen you, not to fill the church coffers."

I'm kidded in our congregation, in fact, for my lengthy preambles that try to defuse every possible objection before I get down to the business at hand. But I'm as anxious for people to know what I *don't* mean as what I do mean.

3. Challenging without condemning.

The last thing I want to do is condemn people. But leadership means challenging people, pointing them to a higher plateau in Christ, sustaining a Philippians 3:13–14 "unsatisfied satisfaction." And the more concerned a pastor is with the deeper dimensions of Christian living—commitment, discipleship, purity of life, devotion to Christ, prayer—the easier it is to dump guilt or condemnation on the flock.

I reviewed the manuscript of another writer recently. He is a younger newcomer to ministry. I noticed that his style was condescending, calling others to growth with phrases such as "Shouldn't we as Christians do better than that?" and "You wouldn't want to fail the Lord, would you?" The article was negative, invoking a sense of failure rather than hope.

I encouraged him, "Turn those phrases around, so you don't invoke defeat or guilt but still call people to be responsible. That would sound something like this: 'With the Holy Spirit indwelling us, we need never fail our Lord Jesus. In him we can do all things!' "

Leading in a Feeding Way

Shepherds lead sheep from pasture to pasture, and so for them, leading is inseparably linked with feeding. I find the same is true for me if I keep the following factors in mind.

Time the challenge

In a Wednesday night service in 1973, a week before Thanksgiving, a man gave a prophetic exhortation about our congregation's future. We were to "intercede for America as if no one else were interceding." (Others were, of course, but we were to pray with a sense of urgency as though no one else was.) At the time, America was embroiled in Watergate and Vietnam, and some journalists were wondering if America would reach its two-hundredth birthday.

I felt the prophetic word forcefully confirmed in my heart, but I didn't act on it immediately. I felt if we tried to launch a new prayer initiative in the middle of the holiday season, people would be too distracted to participate fully. I risked seeming forgetful of this word but felt the long-range call would be better served by a short-range waiting period.

The Lord confirmed my decision. I waited until after the

New Year to follow through. The second Wednesday of January we began 7:14 prayer meetings (based on 2 Chronicles 7:14: "If my people who are called by my name will humble themselves and pray . . ."). We gathered at 7 P.M., as usual, but at 7:14 each week we made extensive intercession for America.

Besides dynamic results in evidence as we prayed, further things happened. Eventually a music group from our church began traveling with the musical "If My People," taking the call to prayer to sixty cities. We underwrote their quarter-million-dollar budget. Over the next two years, other intercessory projects branched off into radio and television, enlisting thousands of other intercessors.

Two decades later, we still offer the 7:14 prayers, but all of that might never have happened if we had tried to lead the people into something new at an unsuitable time.

Pace the challenge

In a congregation of any size, only a percentage will respond immediately to a challenge. In a church of 150, if a pastor leads strongly on an issue, probably thirty at most will respond immediately and enthusiastically. Most will eventually follow, but it will take time.

People are in various degrees of spiritual health; they differ in their ability to hear, capacity to move, and willingness to follow. I can't lead at the pace of the fastest sheep in the flock, leaving behind the aged, the weak, or the sick. I'm obligated to lead the slower sheep as well. Congregations resembling elite marine corps units, which respond at a moment's notice, just don't exist. If I want to bring the maximum number of sheep with me, I must persuade even those who don't bound to their feet at my first call.

Church members won't follow if they doubt they can make it. Climbing into unknown territory is frightening. Although some followers can believe in the value of a leader's vision, they often don't believe they're good enough or spiritual enough to fulfill it. They doubt themselves more than they doubt their pastor's leadership or God's call.

So my leading and feeding will be to no avail unless I believe in my people. I have to believe they would fly if they could, that despite their weaknesses and faults, deep down inside they want to follow Christ. My people will believe in themselves if I lead at a pace they can handle. For example, I am sensitive to how many financial appeals we make per year and how often we ask people to cut extra time in their schedule for special church activities. When they can handle the schedule and their budget absorbs their sacrificial offerings, it gives them confidence.

They'll also believe in themselves if they are being fed. A healthy diet builds strength and brings confidence. Hunger brings a sense of defeat. If they feel defeated and hungry where they are, they'll never go farther.

Sheep follow if they know the shepherd invariably leads to more food. A feeding shepherd, because he or she gains their trust through his servant spirit, only has to give a verbal tug on the heart and the people follow.

For instance, recently our church purchased a church building and grounds located about half a mile from our current church. When the idea for this purchase first came to me two years earlier, I knew it would be difficult for many in our church to accept: "How will we coordinate activities on two separate campuses?" they would rightfully ask. "How will parents drop off their kids in one building and attend church in another, blocks away?" I realized that I would need to prepare the people ahead of time before they could even consider the purchase.

I preached a series of sermons from the book of Joshua on the subject of possessing the land. "God has a promise and a future for each of us and for the church corporately, but we only receive it by going in and taking possession" was my repeated theme.

Months later, when I proposed buying the church to our

leaders and eventually the congregation, the themes of Joshua formed the backdrop. The congregation later followed in this challenging venture because they had been adequately fed beforehand.

This to me is where the two aspects of pastoring come together: we can lead as we feed; we can feed as we lead.

Form enclaves for those who respond at a faster pace

For the "marines" in our church, we provide settings where I can give a stronger challenge. I meet with one hundred young men each month to train them for leadership. I'm not gentle with them. I crowd in tight and hard in that meeting. I say things like "If you don't believe you're supposed to be serving this congregation, don't even come. Those who choose to attend here have made up their minds that we are followers of Jesus Christ. We're serious about prayer, we're in the Word, and we're committed to the church. We know that God wants us serving this particular church."

I'll talk in hard-nosed fashion about what kind of TV programs and movies the men watch, whether they laugh at the off-color jokes at work, how they manage their thought lives, especially their sexual imaginations.

My leadership in this meeting isn't diplomatic or warm, but it is accepted because of the nature of the group.

I can also talk tough with these men because I'm tough on myself—transparent about my own life. I don't address subjects solely in terms of scriptural principles; I tell about my struggles and how I have dealt with them. I don't act as if I have accomplished perfection.

My transparency also cultivates hope among these future leaders. They seem to reason, *Jack means business. He has learned a path of fruitfulness with God, yet he also has struggles just like I do. If he's struggled and overcome, then maybe I can overcome as well.*

Accept the inevitable losses

In the army, when a leader makes a command decision that sends men into battle, he knows there will be casualties. Likewise I know that any church leader's decisions will result in some leaving—seeking a less demanding environment of commitment. I feel that loss deeply. I've never taken casually a person leaving the church. I want to think all our people will sooner or later follow my leadership, but that just isn't reality.

If members choose to leave our church, though, I've come to believe it's because I'm not their shepherd anymore. For whatever reason, they no longer hear the Great Shepherd's voice through me, so I must be content that God has another place for them.

In my early years of pastoral work, when anyone left the church it was terribly painful for me. Most likely, people left both because of my immaturity as a leader and because I served what some regarded as small and undesirable churches.

I know the temptation of struggling to retain people bent on leaving. I also know my personal blind spots, my insensitivities that lead to "losing" people. I think I've overcome impersonal or insensitive ways and found a place of confidence in the Lord, so that if people are committed to leaving, I can "send them with blessing" rather than being pained or declaring them unreliable or disloyal.

Keep in step with the calendar

Our church year begins in September. People return from vacations, and though busy, they are eager for new direction. My opportunity to lead them stretches from the second week in September until the middle of November. I project vision and deliver strength-building exposition at this time.

Holidays consume people's attention from Thanksgiving through the New Year; so I seek to inspire with truth relevant to the season's thrusts.

In January people are inclined to think about new goals and ambitions. That's when diet programs and exercise clubs advertise heavily. In January, I usually focus my preaching on discipleship themes, and in February we emphasize world missions.

Special opportunities come with the Lenten season, as people focus on what Christ has done for them on the Cross and how they should respond. I usually preach on themes like redemption's perfect work, the promise in following Christ, and the person of Jesus.

There is a post-Easter letdown everywhere. I counter this with a strong emphasis in the weeks leading up to Pentecost. Spirit-filled living and resurrection power for service are themes here. We also make a strong emphasis on family and marriage at this time.

In early June we prepare for summer. Even though everyone will be going their separate ways, we find a way to focus on something together, usually by asking everyone to read the same book, devotionally follow the same Bible readings, and memorize the same Scriptures.

Be aware of people's concerns

In January of 1991, I interrupted our church plans because of the Persian Gulf War. Many had family members in the Gulf. Life was upset and they were anxious. When something as prepossessing as war happens, it's time for feeding.

I preached on how we should feel toward someone as hateful as Saddam Hussein, what to do for children watching war reports on television, and how to pray for the troops to be victorious without being vindictive. In addition, we conducted special prayer meetings on the war.

Listen to God's direction

Although I'm attentive to the calendar cycles mentioned above, I don't want to become a slave to the church calendar. God sometimes leads me to do things that counter my assumptions.

Recently, as I was praying over making a financial appeal, I saw in my mind a group of people in a rubber raft being carried through white water. I have never ridden a boat through rapids, so there was no reason for such an image to come to my mind; I felt the vision was from the Lord.

The boat was navigating a canyon with no room on either side to beach. I felt impressed that God was saying our church had a lot of things happening, so it was not the time to add more. We should just hold tight.

That was a difficult decision. Two years earlier we had spent $11 million on a church and campus; people were still affected by that. But if we didn't challenge the congregation financially we would lose a window of opportunity: Easter and a special denominational convention to be held at our church would soon crowd out any church business for several months.

But I decided to go with how I felt God leading me, and several weeks later the Lord guided me to meet this need in another way. I gave myself to several weeks of prayer and then wrote a simple letter of explanation to the congregation.

In effect, I said, "We're all busy, and I haven't the heart to put something else on you. I'm simply asking you to pray and give as you feel directed."

I lead as I feel God directs, but not unless he confirms his direction through our leaders. I never unilaterally follow any impressions regarding the administrative path of the church.

I followed this procedure when our church purchased the church building and campus about half a mile from us.

That process began when I received a literal "word" from the Lord. When I presented the idea to our church, however, I didn't mention what God had revealed to me. If I had done that, the leaders might have been swayed by their trust in me and by my track record of God having led me in the past. Instead I presented the idea first to the elders of the church and to the pastoral staff, then to the 230 deacons, and finally to the congregation.

The elders appointed a task force to study the feasibility of the purchase, a committee from which I absented myself. I

asked them to analyze the purchase without my input. Only after the final decision did I tell the congregation how the Lord
had led me, and this only as an additional witness to them that
God was in our decision. I felt the Lord had indeed led me because *their* faith was aroused without any human manipulation.

The Sunday after the staff member acknowledged to me his
moral failure, I announced to the congregation at the end of our
morning services, "For the first time in my thirteen years as your
pastor, we have had the heartbreaking experience of a moral
difficulty with one of our pastoral team. We will address that
tonight in our evening service."

That night the building was packed. I taught for fifty minutes
on God's perfect design for sexual relationships and why our
disobedience to that design hurts him and us. I explained what
the Bible teaches about leaders who fall, about what their forgiveness does and doesn't mean.

Then we served Communion. With the bread in my hands,
I talked about the brokenness of all our lives but especially how
Jesus was broken on behalf of our brokenness. "What we are
expecting tonight is wholeness," I said.

I took the cup in my hand and talked about the cleansing
power of the blood of Christ.

Before we drank from the cup, I said, "The staff member
who has admitted his moral failure has made clear his intention
to turn from his action and seek restoration within the community life of this church." Then I called him by name to come
forward.

I could hear people quietly weeping all over the auditorium.

He spoke for a few minutes and concluded with, "I ask you
all to forgive me."

After I prayed over the cup, I put my arm around him. I
asked everyone to stretch their hand toward him and in unison
say, "John, I forgive you."

Their voices thundered the response, and we drank from the
cup.

No one could have left that service feeling we had swept his failure under the rug or treated it as unoffensive to God. Nor could anyone leave without feeling a holy reverence for God.

Though always in tension, leading and feeding are not in opposition. When best expressed, we lead when we feed, and we feed when we lead. You can't fully do either alone.

PART 4

Board

15

Maintaining a Healthy Board Relationship

In the official board meeting,
the pastor demonstrates whether he or she is a
dictator or a friend and servant.

—Richard C. Halverson

T he mandate of the Great Commission is not "Go."
Nevertheless, this word has been emphasized so much
that it has overshadowed what happens when one gets there.
It has become a status symbol among evangelicals while the
central words in the Great Commission have been neglected.

"Make disciples" is the mandate. Jesus is the model for such
a ministry. In three years he started a movement that would
reach the whole world and last forever. To accomplish his task
he began by training leaders. Mark records, "He appointed
twelve, that they might be with him, and that he might send
them forth to preach" (Mark 3:14, NASB).

Three years of an intimate, almost unbroken relationship
with Jesus prepared these twelve men to be the nucleus of the
movement that subsequently turned the world upside down.
Their influence continues to this day, nearly 2,000 years later,
to nurture the church Christ is building. Their writings remain
the authoritative source of doctrine for the church; their fellowship the model for Christian unity.

Whether a pastor is starting a new church or beginning his

ministry in an established one, he will find this fundamental strategy of Jesus to be the key for a strong, healthy church with an effective outreach.

The Discipling Pastor

The natural group with which to conduct such a ministry is the church board. Where else could a pastor more wisely begin to disciple? The method is the simple way of Jesus with the Twelve. He ordained them to be with him; he explained everything to them; and he made them his friends, sharing with them things he heard from his Father. Proximity, explaining, and sharing were the basic elements in Jesus' training. Teaching was as much by example as by precept, and common life situations were the classroom. Any pastor will develop and strengthen his relationship with the church board following this simple plan:

First, the pastor must spend time with his board members.

This will not be easy. He is busy, as they are, but there is no substitute for time together. The pastor must make time for this and motivate the board to do the same. A monthly meeting is not adequate in time or atmosphere, but it can be helped greatly by also making time for social fellowship over a meal together or a time of relaxation with the families or a time of simply getting off alone one on one with each member.

When Jesus spent time with the Twelve, their needs began to surface and they became aware of their need of him. It gave Jesus opportunities to deal with their needs on the spot in a natural, relevant way. The disciples learned from what Jesus did as well as from what he said. His attitude under pressure and his response to those who came to him were constant demonstrations of how to care for those in need. Time with Jesus was an ideal "School of the Spirit."

The pastor needs to seek that ideal with the board. At least one spiritual retreat with the board annually is essential. This is not a business retreat, but a time for spiritual renewal. The pastor will likely lead, but occasionally a visiting leader may be in-

vited. The retreat allows a pastor and his board to learn together, grow together, and get to know one another at deeper
levels. It should be a time of corporate, inductive Bible study,
a time for praying together, a time to seek the mind of Christ
together. Each person should have the opportunity to open his
heart, reveal where he is hurting, share his concerns, and allow
others to minister to him. Because it should be a time of reconciliation and authentic fellowship (1 John 1:5–10), some of
the retreat should be structured, but time should also be allowed for informal fellowship. Spouses may be included in
such a retreat with great benefit.

Ideally, the pastor should find time to be with his board
members either individually or a few at a time each week. No
agenda is necessary; the purpose is simply to be with one another. Pastors who meet with board members only when they
have business to discuss don't communicate interest in them as
persons. Rather, a kind of exploitation is communicated suggesting that they are important only as they are useful for some
duty or contribution.

I learned this lesson shortly after I became the assistant pastor at the First Presbyterian Church of Hollywood. Since I
wanted to begin meeting regularly with people on an individual
basis, I first asked a friend if we could spend some time together. He invited me to lunch. We enjoyed the meal and our
visit, but I felt a growing tension, which I later realized was
caused by his wondering when I was going to "make my pitch."

Finally he looked at his watch and said, "Dick, I've got a two
o'clock appointment and must leave in ten minutes. What did
you want?"

"Nothing," I said. "I just wanted to spend some time with
you."

He retorted, "Come on, friend, you can level with me. What
do you want?"

I repeated, "Honestly, nothing; I just wanted to be with
you."

He was silent for a moment; then he said, "Dick, this is the first time a preacher has wanted to be with me when he didn't want something from me."

A significant sequel occurred in my present situation. A new trustee president was elected in my church, and I asked to spend some time with him. We had lunch at his convenience and enjoyed a visit. This time I recognized the growing tension, so I said, "You know, my policy is to be with my brothers as often as possible simply to be with them. If I had something specific to discuss, I would have told you when we made the appointment."

He said, "I heard that was true, but I didn't believe it."

The rest of the time was free from pressure.

The fact is that most laypersons assume that pastors have merely a professional interest in them and desire their company only when their service (or their money) is required for the work. As a result, church boards are rarely much different from the board of directors of a corporation. They simply handle the business—which is a far cry from being undershepherds responsible for the care of the people of God. In contrast, Paul's experience with the elders of Ephesus gives a beautiful picture of the relationship that can exist between elders and pastors and the sense of mission the board can enjoy (Acts 20:28–38).

On the eve of our Lord's betrayal and crucifixion, he gathered the Twelve in the Upper Room where he celebrated the Passover, instituted the Lord's Supper, washed their feet, and gave them a new commandment: "Love one another as I have loved you." Then he added, "By this shall all men know that you are my disciples. . . ." The relationship between pastor and board should manifest such love. Nothing less should be true of those who minister together. It is a wise pastor who gives priority to the nurture of loving, caring, supportive relationships between himself and those with whom he serves. This takes time—much time—but the pastor cannot afford to do less.

Second, that relationship must begin in the official board meeting. There the pastor demonstrates whether he is a dictator or friend and servant, whether he thinks of himself as a member of a team of disciples or the head of an organization that is supposed to run according to his plans. He must understand that he is a servant to the servants of Jesus Christ, who is head and Lord of the church. The board represents the body-at-large whose needs the pastor and board are committed to meet. It is a team ministry in which the head of the church guides and directs not only the pastor but every member of the official board. The pastor should listen much more than he talks and should avoid manipulative practices designed to influence decisions, trusting the Spirit of God to guide the body according to the will of God. Never should the pastor intimidate the board or communicate the idea that they must decide as he wishes. Together they should seek the mind of Christ, which is more likely to be expressed through a consensus than through a simple majority.

This does not mean that the pastor should not have ideas about which way things should go. As a matter of fact, he is responsible for giving leadership to the board. But if he uses threats, intimidation, or ultimatums in the board meetings, he is not exercising authentic leadership. Rather, his influence should come through the friendships he has been nurturing as he disciples them at times other than official meetings. The test for a good idea relevant to the needs of the local church is not its acceptance through coercion, but whether or not it can withstand the prayerful consideration of the board in quiet conversations when there is not the pressure of decision. An idea is like a seed. It must be planted during times of discipleship and allowed time to grow in the hearts and minds of the individuals on the board. When their thoughts have grown to fruition, then let them submit their ideas to the entire board.

Consider having occasional meetings without an agenda. Structure can stifle spontaneity and produce division in a deliberative body. The pressure to make a decision causes minds to be made up before adequate consideration is given to a matter. Create a conversational atmosphere so that all sides of a question may be discussed; then make a decision at a subsequent meeting. This allows time for sufficient reflection before a decision is required.

The pastor who takes his discipling responsibility seriously will implement his task most effectively as he and his board "continually devote themselves to the apostles' teaching and to fellowship, to the breaking of bread and to prayer" (Acts 2:42, NASB).

16

A Crash Course in Conflict

*Much of church conflict is more like championship
wrestling than city riots: it's usually not
as painful as it looks.*

—Gary Fenton

A young leader is angered that the church Bible study she attends is now being taught by a kind but incompetent gentleman. The former teacher, who established and built the class, has been asked by the education director to take a new assignment.

The young leader does not want to see the class dwindle. Nor does she want to be a troublemaker. But she recently attended a seminar on leadership sponsored by her employer; she wants to address the problem.

She does—and sees it escalate from a problem to a conflict. Although the incompetent teacher was removed and the class remained strong, several folks were hurt along the way, including the teacher. But the most lasting impact was on the young leader. She grew negative and judgmental. Although prepared to cope with conflict in the corporate world, she was unprepared to deal with it in her church.

After this happened in our congregation, we added a section in our leadership training on dealing with conflict.

Much of church conflict is more like championship wrestling than city riots: it's usually not as painful as it looks. We cannot prepare church leaders for all types of conflict, so we give them three basic principles that can be adapted to meet the specific situation.

1. *There is a difference between concerned disagreement and conflict.*

Conflict is a disagreement that keeps decisions from being made or the group from moving forward after the decision has been made.

Often leaders fear that any disagreement indicates conflict. A problem or difference of opinion, however, does not mean there is a conflict. There is conflict only when the group cannot make a decision or move forward.

Two years ago in a committee meeting, two strong-willed members had a spirited discussion. The next morning, a concerned young leader called and asked if he could meet with the two people to iron out their differences. We talked through what he had heard. I asked him, "Do you feel the group is ready to make a decision? Did the heated discussion block a decision?"

After some thought, he said it sounded more like *Crossfire* on CNN than a street fight. *Crossfire* is good theater, but it is not conflict. The participants don't quit the show because the debate is spirited.

2. *There is a difference between reconciliation and resolution.*

Resolution usually means finding the answer. Reconciliation means bringing together the folks in conflict. Some issues will never be resolved, but people can still be reconciled.

Often in the process of seeking resolution, however, we compromise and seek middle ground. Many poorly designed church buildings are the result of trying to resolve the conflict between low costs and effectiveness; as a result, neither is accomplished.

A church in East Texas resolved a conflict over stained-glass windows by placing cheap, plastic replicas in its sanctuary. The art crowd will tell you the windows look as if they were purchased at Wal-Mart, and perhaps they were. The pragmatists still resent the fact that because of the windows they had to install extra lighting.

In this instance, the leader tried to help the group make the best decision, then reconcile the people to one another. He had it in reverse. Reconciliation brings people to relational unity but not necessarily to agreement.

A mature gentleman, opposed to the actions of a committee he was on, recently spoke strongly and directly against the committee's recommendation. After the meeting, the mature member sought out the committee's young chairman. It was obvious that the leader had been stung by the intensity of the opposition. The older and wiser man, even though he disagreed with the committee, conveyed his confidence and trust in the chairman. Neither man has resolved with the other his different views on the matter, but they are reconciled.

3. *There is a difference between being peaceful and being a peacemaker.*

A fellow pastor told me about an elected church leader who refuses to become involved with anything controversial. This leader is a no-show on big issues and justifies his behavior as flowing from "a desire to be peaceful."

Being peaceful, however, is different from being a peacemaker, which we are all called to be.

Peacemakers do not sit on their hands; on the contrary, they are often in the middle of conflict, seeking to reconcile leaders. Peacemakers are often risk takers, willing to enter the fray with an expanded heart.

One of our members observed a growing distance between two Sunday school teachers. Their classes attracted the same ages of people and thus competed for new members. The aggressive personalities of the teachers were generating sparks, though there were no brush fires yet.

This member, without waiting for either a full-scale conflict to break out or the permission of the church leadership, met with each leader about the matter. Because of his preventative strike, the conflict was avoided. It also allowed both Sunday school leaders to save their reputations.

17

A Kinder, Gentler Board Meeting

*The boardroom can be a place for spiritual growth.
But it calls for a change in how we approach
our board work.*

—Charles M. Olsen

Have you ever thought about what happens to former church officers? After hearing layleaders say about their term, "I'm glad it's almost over" or "Whew, I made it" or "Never again," I began asking why. I also noticed that a significant number of former church officers became inactive or dropped out of the church.

Recently, *Set Apart Lay Leaders*, a project aimed at revitalizing church boards, polled more than 600 board members. Nearly a third—29 percent—indicated they left "tired, weary, and burned out." They had come asking for bread and were given a stone.

One board member said, "The last three presidents of the church board in our church have dropped out of activity in the church within six months of their term."

Another said, "We were looking for three new council members and went through sixty-three names before we heard our third yes."

What frustrated them about serving on the church board? Here are some comments that reveal deep frustration.

"How burned out I feel. My last year was my most unproductive one."

"How secular it is. We spend more time discussing leaky toilets than why our church is slowly dying due to no growth or vision."

"The lack of interest in pursuing God together. Prayer is a formality, not a way to seek his purpose and plan."

"The lack of concern for seeking Christ's guidance versus following our own personal agendas."

Can serving on a church board truly be life-giving instead of life-draining? Can board meetings actually become "worshipful work"?

Spiritual Focus

I believe board meetings can become worshipful work, and I've devoted the past three years to working with a group of churches to integrate spirituality into their board meetings. One Florida church board commented about the change:

"It is obvious whose meeting this is—it's God's!"

"We are reminded at every point that our service is for God."

"When I go home, I can go right to bed. I used to stay up until midnight unwinding."

"If only the County Board of Commissioners on which I sit could pause for prayer like we do."

The board room can be a place for spiritual growth. But it calls for a change in how we approach our board work. Over time, we have identified four practices that enrich a board.

1. *Storytelling.*

One church council was reviewing its history by recording significant events and names of leaders on a timeline. Someone told the church's founding story: Four German immigrants were playing cards when, in the middle of a hand, one suggested that a new church should be formed in their neighborhood. These Germans rolled up their shirt-sleeves and invited others to share their vision until it became a reality.

After hearing that story, other council members relayed their stories of how they had been invited to the church. The council concluded that a common thread running through the church's history was its inviting character. The council members became so excited that they convened a church meeting. When the people gathered in the fellowship hall, they were greeted with a time line that wrapped around the room. They were invited to record their memories on the timeline and then tell their stories.

The process bonded the council members together, connecting them to the mission of the church and helping them see the importance of what they were doing. Stories do that: they provide a clear identity. Stories bring life and energy. Stories draw out commitment, form community, illuminate personal characteristics and gifts. Often storytelling during a board meeting can clear the air and aid listening, speeding up discussion on issues.

2. *Biblical and theological reflection.*

Mikey was the twelve-year-old mentally handicapped foster son of a family in the process of joining Westminster Church. At a meeting in which the elders were authorizing the baptism of the children in that family, one elder asked, "But what about Mikey?" The elders determined he had a simple love and trust in Jesus.

The day of Mikey's baptism, the congregation was caught off guard when, while being baptized, Mikey burst into a loud, joyful laugh. His beaming smile moved the congregation, which fifteen years earlier had launched a ministry for mentally handicapped children.

Later in a meeting, the session (board) recalled Mikey's baptism. When asked to think of a biblical story or theme triggered by Mikey's story, the session settled on the baptism of the Ethiopian eunuch in Acts 8. In both cases, the baptisms involved elements of surprise. The board members compared the two stories, concluding by telling what they learned.

The session was so excited with the process they asked to continue doing it. Theological and biblical reflection trains board members in the basic beliefs, purpose, and mission of the church.

3. *Prayerful discernment.*

The Presbytery of Cincinnati has adopted a discernment process for its work with sessions of congregations. On certain critical issues, each person on the session prepares a brief statement that is presented to the rest of the board. No debate occurs; neither are weaknesses pointed out. Each person is then asked to go home and pray, searching for the good in each statement.

When the board gathers again, the options are presented and the good in each is highlighted. At this point, each person spends additional time in prayer, searching for the "weightier good."

Finally, the board gathers to seek consensus. If none is found, the board is asked to search their hearts for indifference to God's will. If indifference is found, the process is repeated.

This method of seeking God's will engages all members of the board in prayer. It builds on the wisdom of others, rather than on the ability to point out weak positions. Of course, not every decision can be put to such a lengthy process. But for key decisions, prayerful discernment can turn the board into a center of worshipful work.

One church council was prepared to build a multipurpose gymnasium, since that was what all the growing churches around them were doing. But after slowing down and putting the matter to prayerful discernment, they finally built what they call a "spiritual life center." It's nothing like any Christian education wing or multipurpose gym. As I entered the new building, I noted the number of quiet nooks for conversation or prayer; a small, colorful chapel; a library; a large assembly room. Prayerful discernment led to a unique and fitting solution.

4. *Visioning the future.*

I have conducted a number of retreats for church boards. Halfway into the retreat, I often detect a sigh of relief—most people are relieved to find I don't expect them to paper the walls with newsprint listing all the goals for the coming year, goals that rarely become reality.

Grace United Church is the result of the merger of two declining churches in a declining neighborhood. Their council is made up largely of newer people drawn by the church's neighborhood ministries. They have little money.

When the council spent a day visioning their future, they could not come up with a three-to-five-year plan. In their current situation, they have a hard time envisioning what next year will be like.

Prior to the retreat, the council seemed bound by traditional categories that were strangling their organizational structure. During the retreat they recognized that the natural groupings in the church were already performing the essential functions of worship, nurture, evangelism, and mission. So rather than force committees, they decided to reorganize the church around these natural groupings, training the existing leaders to lead worship, give nurture, and do evangelism and mission.   .

Their vision is to be a celebrative church that cares about its neighborhood. They plan to hold the future God has for them in an open hand and to be open to the gifts God brings. Already God has brought gifts such as youth groups who work in the neighborhood and several people who can speak Spanish. Vision, for them, is a commitment to a direction with mid-course corrections dictated by the opportunities God provides.

Culture of Laughter

As boards have begun to incorporate these four practices, I have seen enormous changes.

Several years ago the pastor and key elders from First

Church in a company town attended a conference called "The Elder as Spiritual Leader." They reported that the corporate ways of the town's company were mimicked in the boards all over town, including the churches'. They wondered if there was a better way. They picked up a few pointers from the conference and went home to work on them.

Recently I visited one of their board meetings. After it was over, they asked what I had observed.

"What you did most and best was laugh," I reported. "You shared fifty-two hearty corporate laughs!"

With that they laughed again, and someone piped up, "Fifty-three . . ." It quickly rose to sixty!

That evening I had also heard thirteen direct expressions of appreciation, seven theological reflections, six references to the Bible, six reports of information, a couple of stories, four hymns, and five pauses for prayer. And four decisions.

I would label this board's culture as a warm family rather than a cold corporation. The members were energized and committed. Serving on that board was no longer life-draining: it was life-giving.

18

Three Key Traits for Your Board

*A shortage of leaders is caused not so much by a
scarcity of good ones as by a scaring
away of the good leaders.*

—Larry Osborne

E very year the nomination committee asks my friend Bob to
run for a term on the church council. Every year he says,
"No, not this year."

Bob would make an ideal board member: He's a mature
Christian and natural leader, and he's committed to the church,
generously supporting it with both time and money. But Bob
remembers the one time he said yes. "The late-night meetings
and arguments were more than I could handle," he recalls. "On
the way home I'd be frustrated and angry, and the next morning
I'd be exhausted at work. Worse, I found myself growing cynical. It took me a couple of years to recover my spiritual equilibrium.

The board at Bob's church was dysfunctional. The symptoms are easily recognized: frequent tardiness, absenteeism,
and a perennial problem securing enough qualified people
willing to serve. The predictable result is a chronic leadership
crisis—a shortage caused not so much by a scarcity of good
leaders as by a scaring away of the good ones.

Over the years, I've served on, worked with, or been around
many dysfunctional boards. I've noticed that in almost every

instance there has been a conspicuous lack of three traits. In contrast, these same three traits dominate the decision-making process when a board is healthy and effective. So I've made their development a top priority.

Teamwork

As any sports fan knows, the best players don't always win the championship. The best team does. What's true on the field is also true in the boardroom. When everyone knows, accepts, and fulfills his role on the leadership team, the odds for success escalate.

I've found there are two common saboteurs of teamwork: lack of a clearly defined leader, and failure to distinguish between designing and evaluating a ministry.

One thing every team needs is a clearly defined leader. Teamwork depends on it. Someone has to keep the group headed in the same direction.

I compare the leader to a point guard on a basketball team. Directing the offense falls on his shoulders. That doesn't mean the shooting guard, forwards, or center can't initiate a play or fast break, but most of the time they'll look to him to take the lead. In a church, a leader sets the agenda, general tone, and direction for ministry. When a tough problem or exciting opportunity comes along, everyone knows to whom to look for direction.

This type of leader is very different from an authoritarian leader. An authoritarian leader expects to be obeyed; an initiating leader expects to be heard. Once he's made his point, he leaves it up to the team whether to accept, modify, or reject his advice. He's what my friend Charles Bradshaw calls a "powerful servant." In other words, he's a leader, not a monarch.

In most cases, the senior pastor is the person best suited for this position. But obviously there are times when a church's polity, history, or other factors make that impossible or inadvisable. What's important is that one person leads. Dysfunctional boards tend to have two or three people vying for the leadership position, resulting in attacks on one another rather than on the problems at hand.

I realize some people advocate a leaderless board as the ultimate expression of unity and teamwork. I once counted myself among them. But I think I erred on two counts.

First, I failed to acknowledge the role of *de facto* leaders. What I called a "leaderless board" was often far from leaderless. For instance, I know of one church that prided itself on not having an officially designated leader. But sanctioned title or no, it was obvious who the real leader was—so much so that most people said, "I go to Gene Johnson's church." As long as Gene was around, the "leaderless" board worked marvelously. His charisma, knowledge, and arbitration skills kept everyone headed in the same direction. But once Gene left, so did the board's teamwork. Within two years they were embroiled in controversy.

Second, I underestimated the fury of a storm. When a crisis hits a church, people need to know who's in charge. As long as there's smooth sailing, there is no great need for a captain; anyone can man the helm. But once a storm hits, someone has to take charge, and when he does, it's important the crew has no qualms about his ability or right to lead.

Settling on a clearly defined and accepted leader is one of the first steps to greater teamwork.

Something else that can sabotage teamwork is the failure to distinguish between designing and evaluating.

Designing is a solo task; it needs to be carried out by one person (or at the most two or three). Evaluating, on the other hand, is a group task; the more the merrier.

When an entire board tries to design, create, or generate new programs, it's headed for failure and frustration. There are good reasons why people joke about planning by committee. It's no accident that the world's greatest inventions, musical compositions, and artistic masterpieces have come from inspired individuals, not blue-ribbon committees.

At Bob's church, whenever a crisis or golden opportunity loomed, his pastor came to the board and said, "What do you think we ought to do?" That put the board in an impossible position. With thirteen members, they were too large and diverse a group to develop an effective proposal. Most of the time, after pooling ideas, they'd argue late into the night over how to combine them into a workable plan. Eventually they'd table the discussion until the next meeting.

Teamwork doesn't mean everybody does everything; it means everyone does what he does best. Translated to a board setting, it means letting the leader, staff, or a small group propose strategy. Then the entire group can evaluate, fine-tune, and modify the plans—things larger groups do well.

We've learned to strenuously avoid designing by committee. In fact, we have no standing committees outside of our elder board. When we have a problem or opportunity, we turn it over to an individual or *small* group: a pastor, a staff member, a fellow elder, or a task force. We leave it to them to propose an innovative solution.

Once the designers have a proposal, the board moves into action. We evaluate. If anything is wrong or missing, we can usually find it. Sometimes we even scrap the idea and move in an entirely new direction. But the key to the board's effectiveness is having something to react to rather than trying to work from a blank slate.

For a church board to fully experience teamwork, I believe it needs to accept that initiating and designing ministry are individual skills, while evaluating and critiquing are group skills. Then the board can allow individuals to do what they do best, and concentrate on the group activities it does best. The result? Shorter meetings, less frustration, and a more innovative ministry.

Courage

A second mark of a healthy board is courage. When a tough decision has to be made, people aren't afraid to make it. They realize that's what they've been called to do. In contrast, dysfunctional boards often are dominated by fear. They find it safer to say no and to maintain the status quo.

Why do some boards lack courage? One, groups tend to be more conservative than individuals, more cautious and oriented toward the past. Two, most board members take their responsibilities as a sacred trust. They are hesitant to take unnecessary chances, alienate members, or make a mistake. These are commendable concerns, but when taken to an extreme they can paralyze the decision-making process.

I've found that whenever a board lacks the courage to lead, it tends to lean too heavily upon two opinion-gathering devices: (1) surveys, and (2) congregational meetings.

Surveys seldom give us the accurate information we think we're getting. Not long after I arrived at this church, I used a survey to gauge interest in small-group Bible studies. I was thrilled to discover over half the congregation wanted to be in one. I gathered leaders, and we put together a series of studies. However, when it came time to sign up, hardly anyone did. Only later did I realize what had happened. People had answered my survey with what they perceived to be the "right answer." They felt they ought to be in a Bible study, so they hesitated to check the box saying "No, I won't be able to participate."

Another problem with surveys is that by nature they zero in on what people want, not what they need. Ask a group what to study next and invariably you'll find prophecy and a host of controversial subjects at the top of their list. Teaching on prophecy is hardly most people's greatest need. A pastor who planned his preaching schedule around such surveys would be derelict in his duties as a spiritual leader. The same goes for a board that relied too heavily upon opinion polls when making decisions or designing a ministry.

Another tool that can be misused is congregational meetings. I'm not talking about an annual meeting or a constitution that puts ultimate authority in the hands of the congregation.

That's the system my church uses, and I'm not only comfortable with it—I also advocate it. My concern is with situations in which the leaders turn all but the most significant decisions back to the congregation. I realize that questioning the effectiveness of congregational meetings is, to some, tantamount to heresy. But I wonder if asking an entire congregation to be intricately involved in the decision-making process is the best way to do things. It's a sure way to increase the likelihood of conflict and division.

In all but the smallest churches, it's unreasonable to expect everyone to come to the meetings. As a rule of thumb, the larger the congregation, the smaller the percentage of people who show up. As a result, it's easy for a small faction of chronic complainers and malcontents to wield an inordinate amount of power.

That's what happened at Ron's church. In the early years, the small flock met once a month to hammer out issues and okay expenditures. It worked so well they wrote it into the constitution. Forty years later they still held a congregational business meeting on the first Wednesday of every month. Hardly anyone showed, but those who did haggled over every nickel and dime, in essence holding hostage a church of four hundred. Why didn't the rest of the congregation show up and put an end to it? They (1) lacked the time, (2) hated meetings, (3) abhorred conflict, and (4) trusted their elected leaders. So they tried to ignore the undercurrent of hostility, hoping it would go away.

Those who champion lots of churchwide business meetings assume that the more people involved in the decision-making process, the better the final decision will be. But there is no way an entire congregation can work through a complex issue as carefully as a small board. The result will almost always be more heat than light.

That's why our board never asks the congregation to debate a number of options. Instead, we bring a single proposal and ask the people to approve or reject it. This is true whether it's our annual budget, a proposed addition to our staff, or any other item.

We believe it's our job as leaders to dig through the facts, compare the consequences of various options, and come up with a plan. Then it's the congregation's prerogative to accept or reject that plan. That's not to say we don't give the congregation an opportunity to offer input or ask tough questions. But it's our goal to get any debate, concerns, or proposed changes on the table long before the congregation gathers to vote.

We accomplish this in a couple of ways. First, we inundate people with Sunday announcements and congregational letters to make sure they know exactly what we are proposing and why. Second, we hold question-and-answer sessions a few weeks before the meeting so everyone can make suggestions, register complaints, or clarify issues. Frankly, not many people show up at these informational meetings. But the meetings give people a place to vent feelings, and they give us an opportunity to interact with critics away from the emotionally charged setting of a congregational meeting.

The result? Boring congregational meetings. Most last ten to fifteen minutes. I can't remember the last time someone raised his voice or got mad. We've found that most church members want the board to lead. They have no desire to get mired in the sticky details, and they don't like the confusion, conflict, and inefficiency of large-group decision making. As long as they have opportunity for input and the authority to say yea or nay on major decisions, they're happy.

Healthy boards realize this and lead. If we're going to develop courage in our board, we need to help the board not to shift its leadership back to the congregation.

Trust

The final key trait I want our board to display is trust. Every board I've worked with has had a basic bent toward either trust or suspicion. Dysfunctional boards ask "Why?" Healthy boards ask "Why not?"

What made the difference? In most cases it was a choice. Dysfunctional boards chose the role of watchdog, making sure no one got by with anything. Predictably, they had an abundance of adversarial relationships. On the other hand, healthy boards chose trust.

How can we develop trust in our board?

To begin with, by helping the board avoid micromanagement. A consuming attention to detail reveals only one thing: lack of trust in the competence and judgment of others. A board develops trust as it keeps its focus on the big picture—setting direction, making policy. Trusting boards don't argue over what kind of tires to put on the church van. They leave that decision to the people who maintain and drive the van.

One friend served on a board that insisted upon approving every expenditure over ten dollars. They spent so much time on the budget they never had time for the more important issues—prayer, strategy, and vision.

Overattention to the details of ministry creates a bottleneck. Nothing gets done until the board has a chance to meet. For those on the front lines that can be incredibly frustrating, particularly when they need to make a decision or a purchase *now*. It creates a perception that the board is an obstacle to progress, something to get around—an enemy rather than an ally.

Micromanagement also tends to undercut creativity. By definition, a creative idea goes against the grain. It's different from "the way we've always done things." But by the time micromanagers have finished with an idea, it's usually rather conventional. For example, the pastor of a neighboring church wanted to know why home fellowships had worked well for us. He wanted to start some. I was careful to point out that much of the success was due to some creative twists we'd given the program. Later, I found out that his board had liked the idea, but unfortunately they were micromanagers. By the time they were finished reworking the idea, not one of the unconventional aspects was left. The result was a plain-vanilla program that never excited anyone.

Sometimes in the early days of a ministry, micromanagement is a necessity. But as a church grows, the board needs to move away from managing details to overseeing the big picture. This transition depends on their willingness to trust others.

Healthy boards give people freedom to do things in whatever way they deem best. In matters of taste, style, or methodology, they don't butt in. They let those who have the responsibility for a ministry also have the authority to carry it out.

The Hessian mercenaries understood this principle as well as anyone. The three guiding principles in their Rules of Combat would serve any board well.

1. *The mission's objective and any constraints must be made explicit by the commander [the board] in advance.*

In other words, everyone has to know the rules ahead of time—both the goal and the limits of their freedom. For instance, our youth associates need to know how we're going to judge the success of their program. Will it be by attendance, number of new Christians, sign of spiritual growth, or the percentage of church kids that buy in? And what are their constraints? Do they have a budget? How much? Are there any programs or ministries they must provide (Sunday school, camps, or a set number of socials)?

Any good job description will do. What's important is that both staff and key volunteers know explicitly what the board expects them to accomplish.

2. *Individuals are to be given the freedom to pursue the objective as they think best in the light of local conditions.*

No one knows better than those on the front line what will and won't work. Most of us have had the experience of being forced to do something in a way that we knew was less than

best. I remember once being forced to use a certain speaker,
who I knew would be boring, at a conference I was planning.
Worse, I had to emcee the meetings and introduce the speaker.
That put me in a compromising position. If I promoted the conference, knowing full well our people would get little or nothing out of it, my credibility would suffer. If I downplayed the
conference, and no one came, I'd have a financial disaster on
my hands. Needless to say, the board's interference was not appreciated.

This principle is particularly important when dealing with
staff. Why hire an expert if we aren't going to let him do his
thing? When our board hires someone, we look for the wisest
and most gifted person we can find. For us to kibitz and control
the details of the ministry would waste his or her gifts and indict
our judgment in hiring.

3. The freedom of officers [ministry leaders] is to be limited only when it's essential in order to coordinate their actions.

Keeping everyone moving in the same direction is one of
the board's primary jobs. Sometimes that calls for reining in a
particular ministry. I know of one church where the music program became so large that the splashy programs and travel
tours left few volunteers for anything else. So when the director
asked for permission to raise funds for another bus and still
more sound equipment the board had to say no.

Occasionally, a special emphasis or program will also mandate that freedom be temporarily set aside. During a missions
emphasis we can't have the youth group off on a ski trip, or the
women's ministry hosting a weekend retreat. But other than
times like these, it's hands off. Even if we doubt an idea will
work, we try to give people the freedom to give it a shot. That's
what trust is all about.

19

Bringing Out the Best in Your Board

Showing honor and deference to the board is one way we enhance the dignity of an institution.

—David Hubbard

A relationship of integrity between the leader and the board is crucial. Members of the board must be able to say no to the leader. The leader must respect their authority enough that if the board says no, he or she will make one of two choices: resign or say yes to the board's will.

You cannot have a board whose authority you defy.

I have never been too frustrated by board structures. They come with the territory, and I believe in them deeply for several reasons.

First, if the leader enables the board to be a good board, the board then enables the organization to minister effectively.

Second, good organizations spread power. When the power is spread, the board sees itself at the bottom of the pyramid, not the top. Rather than thinking the pastor is at the top with the board beneath, or the board at the top with the pastor beneath, we see the mission at the top of the pyramid with the rest of the organization next, supported by the board.

Boards serve an essential purpose: They're required by law for organizations. If a corporation owns property or pays employees, a board is responsible for the adherence to the rules and regulations of each state.

Beyond that accountability, the board represents the organization to the community, giving it credibility and a sense of integrity. A board brings support, vision, and something many people don't think about—continuity. Leaders change at some point, and the board is responsible for succession. The board is the group committed to the continuity of the organization's ministry.

Showing honor and deference to the board is one way we enhance the dignity of an institution. An institution that does not treat board members well is like a family that doesn't honor its parents. To the extent that board members are manipulated or finessed, to the extent a leader makes end runs around them or doesn't take their will and wishes seriously, to that extent the dignity of the institution is compromised. Board members lose motivation, and the staff's accountability to the trustees is degraded.

Here are some ways I try to bring out the best in the board I lead.

Believer Selection

In prospective board members, we look for people who already believe in our organization. I never want to use the board as a way of getting people's interest. I've tried that before, and it doesn't work. It backfires because it doesn't have integrity. I look for loyalty, for someone who has already started to give, for somebody who is already on the way.

Second, I want to know how a person uses power. People who want the board position because it will give them power differ from people who want the board position because it gives them the opportunity to serve and grow. So I try to find out how someone behaves when they "lose." Everybody on the board loses at some time or another. At that stage, if they pick up their marbles and leave, they aren't good board members. Knowing how to lose gracefully and maintain their loyalty when their peers have out-voted them is an essential element of their Christian maturity.

Of course, such things must be discovered about a person before he or she is in the fires of board conflict. We learn about people by being in their homes, talking to them, talking to people who know them; by visiting their place of business, seeing how they treat the staff; by seeing whether they are process persons or Lone Rangers.

Lone Rangers may be wonderful contributors to an organization, but they don't always make good board members. They are accustomed to making suggestions that others implement. People who have worked more in corporate or educational life are used to negotiating. Surgeons don't negotiate much! (Although many medical people have made fine board members.) Persons who work where they largely have full authority need to be checked out to make sure they know when they lead and when they don't lead. That requires knowing them well.

Sometimes a church nominating committee is pressured by others in the congregation to nominate someone who has been in the church twenty years but doesn't meet these standards. In such cases the pastor must remind the committee what the essential question is: Will he or she be a good elder? If the answer is no, then it's incumbent upon the staff and the lay leadership to find other roles for those people that honor their seniority.

Many of those who would not make good board members would make good independent consultants. Staff members can have breakfast with Charlie Jones, saying, "This is what we're thinking. You have been here a long time; you have a sense for the history of the church. What would your counsel be? What are the strengths and weaknesses of this proposal? What should we watch out for?" You can use those people without putting them in a situation where they have to negotiate, compromise, and fit in with a group.

A board has to see itself as a team. It doesn't have to agree on everything, but it has to trust the decision-making process.

Roles Played

Good trusteeship carries a lot more with it than simply being at the meetings.

First, when board members vote, they are governors. The right group makes basic decisions in a proper manner. Decisions are not ad-libbed or ad-hocked. This keeps the process tidy, orderly—and legal!

Second, board members are consultants. Each board member will have areas of expertise and special experience. The consulting role will often be exercised outside the board meeting.

Because of his profession and aptitude, our board chairman, Sam Reeves, is the most important financial consultant we have at Fuller. But he doesn't talk a lot about that at board meetings. Occasionally he will give a rundown on what he thinks is going on in the economy, but he helps us most over the phone with the key financial players. The same is true with our board members who are lawyers, developers, business managers, or professional educators.

The third role of board members is ambassador, which means representing us. They represent us with a constituency, with a particular group that they are close to. They help interpret what the institution is doing. They defend it when it is under pressure. They bring feedback on how it is perceived.

The fourth role board members play is sponsor. They give of themselves and encourage others to give. We say to those we recruit, "We expect you to give proportionate to your means and to assign a high priority to our institution."

To get a board to work well is labor-intensive. You could put all this in a job description, but it may never get off the page unless the leader takes the initiative. Most trustees of churches are busy and hesitant to impose themselves. But they are waiting to be asked.

Board Care

It's my job to see that board members do not lose interest in their responsibilities. Good people don't want to be part of an organization in which they are not asked to contribute or their contribution is not recognized. Volunteers need to be drawn into the center of the organization. Every organization needs a strong center, but people will only be drawn into the center if the demand is made and if they are supported in the fulfillment of that demand. They will serve wonderfully if they are challenged and helped. Henrietta Mears said, "Never let a volunteer fail."

We want to make a board meeting an event. Our board chairman wants us to experience community as we share ourselves and taste the joy of life together.

The payoff for board members comes at a couple of places. One is that they grow personally. This happens, among other ways, by bringing in experts who talk about something that will help board members grow.

The other payoff is joy. We want each member to say that it has been good to be with these people. We can have that joy even when dealing with tough situations because Christ is present. A spirit of love, honesty, and integrity while handling issues can feed joy even when the news itself is not as bright as we would like it to be.

Leaders need to coach people to view the board as a ministry rather than an obligation. Start by improving the spiritual and intellectual relationship among board members. If I were moving into a pastorate, I would make Bible study, personal sharing, and prayer times with the board a high priority. I would seek times when they could be weak, honest, and vulnerable with one another. I would also try to model that.

You might have to start with three or four people within the group who are more open to this practice. Begin a weekly breakfast with that group to lay out your vision. Help them see the board not as the way the church does its business but as the model of the church in prayer, study, and service.

Meeting Prep

The missing ingredient in most church board meetings is planning. A board meeting has to be structured to enable people to contribute. Getting the board members' contribution is the most important single goal. Find issues with which they can become involved: wrestling with problems, seeking out possibilities, and promoting ideas. Do some "blue sky" thinking so board members feel they have done more than come, listen, and vote. When the meeting ends, people need to know the ministry is different because they made the effort to be there.

Planning starts with the pastor and the chair of the board (or whoever is the appropriate layleader in that congregation) sitting down together and figuring out the three or four most important things to accomplish at that meeting. If they plan accordingly, the board meetings will not be laundry lists of activities or times for reading off report after report. Anything that can be mailed out and read in advance ought to be handled that way. Board members should not have to sit through a meeting having reports read to them.

Keep meetings on track by using a timed agenda. The standard criticism of church meetings is that they're too long. They are too long because nobody weighs the relative value of the various issues and suggests the amount of time each item is worth. In this instance, Parkinson's Law takes over: the amount of discussion becomes inversely proportional to the importance of the issue. We take an hour on the color of the wastebasket and just ten minutes on something crucial for the ministry of the church.

The role of the chairperson or moderator is to keep the meeting focused. Time is wasted when the focus gets blurry. If this happens, the chair needs to say, "Let's focus on the issue. Here's what's before us as I see it."

Another responsibility of the chairperson is to test the support of an idea. If people can register their support, then you can promptly end the discussion and move on to the next component. But the chair has to read the climate and be sure all sides are heard from. The chair needs to watch body language. The chair may say, "It looks to me like most of you are with this proposal, but I'm not sure what I am reading from you (to a particular member). Do you want to share with the group what you are feeling?" Good chairing makes time productive and still gives people a chance to express their convictions.

Conflict Handling

Years ago when we were choosing an architect, one trustee was a strong advocate for a certain world-class designer, but another trustee criticized this person's work. This made the one trustee so angry he left the meeting and walked around the block.

When he came back, he asked to speak to the board. He said he was learning that we have these tensions because we care so much. Rather than seeing the tensions as bad behavior, we can see them as the expression of personal investment. To care too much and to lose a little control over your tongue may be healthier than having people who could care less about how things go.

While disagreements are part of the process on a healthy board, we can do several things to minimize harmful conflict. Sometimes we need to take a break. Try to talk with people during the break to help them clarify the issues. Sometimes we will ask a person to write out their concerns so we can address them specifically.

But if it gets too hot, break off and give a little space. Often people will get together and work differences out by themselves. Or the person will cool down and apologize after the break. Just allowing a little breathing room with good people usually takes care of any bad feelings.

Occasionally we need to delay a decision. We had to do this with the inclusive-language issue. A dozen people felt strongly about it and were articulate. At any given point we could have gotten the vote, but Sam and I have always felt there are some things more important than getting the vote. At some point you have to vote and get on with it, but you don't want the vote to tear the place up.

Indeed, this issue threatened to tear us up. We had many public discussions, and I had whole days of private communication with some people. They weren't only being mean or obstreperous or causing trouble; they were agonizing over it. On one occasion, Sam bought an airline ticket in order to spend hours with one trustee who was in terrible personal pain over this issue. Sam let him know he was loved and valued, and heard him out. This trustee's view of God was at stake. He was waging a spiritual battle.

That issue was on the front burner for at least two years. Eventually we did have to bring closure to it by taking a vote. We had about four negative votes out of thirty people, but it cleared the air. Nobody has brought it up again; nobody has harked back to it as a time when we made a great mistake.

When someone votes against the majority and obviously feels strongly about the issue, I try to make immediate contact with that person after the meeting. If somebody has been wounded by a board decision, it is important to reach them as soon as possible to see how they're doing. Don't avoid them. I often go and hug that person after the meeting or at the next break.

As painful as it is, conflict can help the organization if handled properly. Before the 1980 presidential election, Rev. Jerry Falwell and his Moral Majority were getting a lot of attention from the press. I told the executive committee that I wanted to distinguish between where I was and where we were as a seminary in relation to the emphases that Dr. Falwell was putting forth.

Some board members felt more closely drawn to the Moral

Majority approach than I did. Frankly, they thought I was out
in left field, and I felt they didn't fully understand the situation.
I was pained over that and somewhat depressed for a while because I had thought we were closer in our viewpoints. Yet it
was probably my fault. I had not done as good a job in mentoring the trustees as I thought.

I had been surprised, hurt, and angry, but out of that tension, I decided to act constructively and began to write the
drafts of what became our Mission Beyond the Mission Statement. We spent almost three years discussing what Fuller cared
about beyond the training of evangelical leadership in our three
main areas (theology, psychology, and missions). We were able
to build consensus around that document. It has helped us
know what our margins are, what range of opinions we can tol-
erate. Along with our mission statement and statement of faith,
it has given us another screening device to test whether faculty
members and trustees will fit.

I thought it was important to involve others in the process
of drafting that statement. I drafted it first, but the statement
went through ten drafts before it was published. What I do in
such situations is include every idea that possibly can be included from board members, staff, and faculty members.

We as leaders don't want to narrow the work of an institution to the shape and size of our own vision. It is our task to be
vision-sparkers, vision-gatherers, vision-organizers, and vision-
sorters. Every congregation, every board, if it's any good at all,
has more vision than can possibly be put to work. The leader's
responsibility is to bring out the best of that vision. The vision
is a corporate activity. In theological terms, the vision is an exercise in the communal life of the body of Christ and the shared
practice of the gifts of the Spirit.

Leader Production

It's the little things that help leaders work successfully with
a board. I try to know the board members well, to be familiar

with their families and businesses. I need to know them, their pain, what's going on in their lives. I try to be there at their times of special need. And I need them to know where I am, what I'm struggling with, what I need to do. The little things come out of seeking to know one another well.

Can a pastor justify spending so much time and energy with a limited group of people in the church? I think so. Although you pastor the board with an intensity you can't possibly give even a tenth of the congregation, this builds into the congregation a nurturing pattern that spreads and catches almost everybody.

If developing and nurturing leadership is important, then the important thing is not only that the board gets its work done. Pastors have an opportunity for personal influence on the members of that board unlike that which they may have on any other group in the church. What better place for nurturing leadership gifts? Pastors can urge people forward, encouraging them to do what they didn't think they could, enabling people to take steps toward maturity in Christ. They are then equipped so others will follow them in the steps of our Lord.

While I consider relationships within the board as important as their votes, I haven't always maintained as good a balance as I'd like. Most leaders are more agenda-driven than relationship-driven. If you win the issues but lose the people, you lose. If you succeed in getting buildings built or programs set up or money raised, but you leave a lot of wounded in the field, that's not good. You have to keep moving toward the target, but you only reach that target if people believe in it and help you reach it. Everything we do that amounts to anything is done through and for people.

PART 5

Individual

20

Person-Centered Motivation

*We all shift into high gear when we're praised for what
we're already doing well.*

—Ruth Senter

Y ou've seen the man.
Amid his regalia of red, white, and blue, he points a bony
finger directly into your line of vision, shatters your complacency with his piercing stare, and shouts his message without
saying a word: "Uncle Sam Needs You."

Compelling figure that he is, his lavish guarantees of seeing
the world, on-the-job training, and career security do not move
more than a handful of people to cross his threshold and sign
on the dotted line. Lack of patriotism? Uninformed about the
needs? Faulty recruitment? Who knows? But somehow, despite
his panorama of persuasion, Uncle Sam often fails to recruit.

The church and Uncle Sam face a common dilemma—enlisting recruits. Although there are any number of reasons why
Uncle Sam has to work hard at it, one cannot help but ask why
the church, of all places, suffers from an acute case of man-
power anemia.

Recruitment Puzzle

Why is it that recruitment is often listed as the number-one
source of frustration for the Christian education director? Why

do many leaders feel that finding enough people to staff their programs is a task as difficult as scaling Mount Everest? Why are members reluctant to join the service ranks; or, once they do join, why the fatalities along the way? What about Christ's call to service? Is it not clear? Or the sense of mission—does it not inspire sacrificial commitment to a program?

Certainly the problem can't be traced to a shortage of recruitment tools. We have as many how-to-do-it plans as there are flies at a summer picnic. Recruitment manuals abound—written by Christian educators who theorize, systematize, and publicize fresh approaches to this age-old problem. Check the bookshelves of any local C.E. director and you will find at least a dozen books on recruitment.

Know-how is not the bottleneck.

Neither is our theological framework. The structure for the discovery and use of spiritual gifts within the church is solid. Spiritual-gift inventories uncover rich deposits—stockpiles of resources to feed recruitment programs. But despite all the gold we have discovered in the spiritual gift mine, churches are still volunteer-poor.

We have even developed several very fine recruitment procedures. We issue consistent, clear appeals that prod our membership toward the volunteer ranks. Sermons abound on stewardship. Human Resource Surveys canvass the membership twice a year. We call for signatures during a yearly time-and-talent faith-promise campaign. Recruitment committees follow up the leads. Lunch at the Holiday Inn comes compliments of the Christian education director and the church budget. We have spared neither energy nor funds on our enlistment programs.

Why then do church leaders have to work so hard at uncorking bottled-up resources?

Possibly the missing piece in the recruitment puzzle is the leaders' lack of understanding of motivational factors, those inner drives and needs that move people to action.

How do you discover what motivates a potential recruit?

How do you capitalize on a person's motivation once you discover it? How do you create conditions that will continue to keep the fires fueled? Is it possible to create niches of service that will serve the needs of both the organization and the individual?

The New Motivations

Rick was a likely candidate to lead the teen choir. His application for church membership displayed impressive credentials: a master's degree in composition, a music teacher in a public school system. "Directing musical groups" was one of the things he listed under "like to do most." As a new arrival in the community, he saw the church not only as an opportunity for spiritual enlargement but also as a launching pad for fresh relationships.

Rick was not a reluctant recruit. He prayerfully considered his contribution to the church as he checked "music" on the Human Resource Survey. When the youth director took him to lunch and described the need for a teen choir, Rick agreed that his past experiences pointed him toward directing the teen choir. He said yes, planned his strategy, and went to work.

As time passed, however, a discomfiting fog settled over Rick's commitment to his volunteer job. He couldn't define his feelings, nor could he find a basis for them. The choir had come a long way. He was pleased with most of their performances and suspected that the church staff was impressed with his work. Yet, even though he enjoyed the kids, they were of another time and place. His own high school days seemed long ago and far away. He felt more and more isolated and lonely. Those fresh relationships that he had envisioned with peers never materialized. He felt compelled to do his job well, but it left him little time and energy for other pursuits in the church.

Rick didn't quit his job with the teen choir—he was too conscientious for that. When he considered writing a letter to the youth director telling of his need to develop relationships with church people his own age, he felt selfish and guilty. His need for companionship seemed too trivial. No crises were unsettling his life, so he didn't schedule a session with the pastor. Since no one ever asked, he never bothered to unload his feelings.

After a year and a half, Rick simply left the church. "Maybe at the next place I can find room to serve and still get to know people my own age," he wrote his mother when he told her about his change in churches.

A professional church tramp? Uncommitted? Maybe. But the point is, no one asked about needs—his needs. The need for a director for the teen choir was the major consideration. Had someone thought of asking, "What rewards do you hope to receive from serving the church?" or even, "What do you fear the most about directing the teen choir?" Rick's story might have had a different ending.

Questions about motivation must be asked. Industry has perceived the problem. Psychologists and researchers have also made some significant observations that the Christian educator would do well to consider in his thoughts and plans for recruitment.

In a discussion on "The New Job Values" (*Psychology Today*, May 1978), Daniel Yankelovich, research professor of psychology at New York University, links the issues of motivation to job incentives. "Millions today find job incentives so unappealing that they no longer are motivated to work hard. As a result, they withdraw emotional involvement." Yankelovich blames this withdrawal on the fact that the "old incentive system has failed to catch up with new motivations." The incentives of the '50s and '60s—money, status, rewards, fringe benefits—no longer work.

According to Yankelovich and other dissectors of trends, America is turning inward. She has shifted her value system from external rewards to an internal sense of fulfillment. Self-actualization motivates people today—not money. The philosophy of the new breed of workers is, "I am more than my role."

Yankelovich issues his mandate: "Revamp incentives to fall in line with new motivations."

What are the new motivations? *Psychology Today* researchers Patricia Penwick and Edward Lawler decided to find out. From the 28,000 readers of the magazine who responded to their questionnaire about job values, most stated that external rewards—money and status—were not motivational, but psychological satisfactions were personal growth, a sense that *they* are worthwhile, and a feeling of accomplishment. Abraham Maslow coined the phrase *self-actualization*—a need to become all that one has the potential of becoming. According to Maslow, self-actualization ranks as the highest category of needs as well as the category that can be most easily left unfulfilled.

Psychological fulfillment—the new motivation?

Self-Actualization Breakdown

So what should the church be doing about it? One possibility is to stuff it into a box marked "self-centeredness" and store it on a shelf along with all the other unusable secular philosophies. For the Christian, motivation to serve comes from the Holy Spirit, not from some slick psychologist who understands people well enough to con them into doing what he wants them to do. Motivational psychology, we might think, smacks of manipulation; and when church leaders try to move people, are they not counterfeiting the Holy Spirit? Playing God is a dangerous game.

The warning is valid. If the success of a church's volunteer program depends solely on the psychological fulfillment of its workers and the ability of its leadership to be people-movers, it will fail. If the direction and guidance of the Holy Spirit is not a primary consideration in the recruitment and maintenance of volunteer staff, the church might as well be General Motors.

However, recruiting volunteers without looking at the relevant psychological principles is very much like driving a car without having the faintest idea what's under the hood. Sooner or later there will be breakdowns we won't know how to handle.

Although he had seminary training, was ordained, and was a theoretician *par excellence,* when it came to education in the church, Joe knew little about personnel breakdowns. I worked for Joe once. He was a master at his job; he ran committee meetings with the precision of a commanding officer—timed agendas, goals, objectives, evaluations, implementation. He moved us through massive doses of church-school business painlessly. Order and efficiency distinguished his team. We all knew where we'd been, where we were going, and how we were going to get there.

What we didn't know was anything about Joe. He seemed as cold and distant as the moon. We saw him in action; we respected his know-how; but that's as far as it went. Joe knew about us—Primary II, Table 3, eleven o'clock hour; piano player; storyteller; scriptwriter; former children's club leader; can type sixty words a minute. What more did you need to know about your volunteers to run an efficient church-school program?

Joe conversed well with his workers as long as the discussion had to do with business. But his "Hi, how's it going?" never quite did the trick when it came to personal matters. Joe never asked about our goals, dreams, hopes, fears, past successes or failures, families, or feelings toward our church job.

Interestingly, Joe's programs always had "Vacancy" signs over them. Commitment to Joe's team was short-lived. Some of us lasted twelve months; others faded sooner. What Joe never understood was that it takes more than technical efficiency to outfit a team; more than a perfect match between task and spiritual gift to keep job satisfaction at a high level; and more than clearly defined goals and objectives to keep workers motivated. Even though he was a genius at outer dynamics, Joe never understood the dynamics at work inside of people. As a result, his team kept falling apart.

Church leadership cannot ignore the psychological dynamics that move people and keep them committed. How, then, can church leadership provide a climate where workers' needs for self-actualization are met, while their needs to donate time and work to the church are met also? Can it be done?

People Over Programs

Don is proof that it can be done. No one knows for sure what it is that keeps people volunteering year after year to work under Don's leadership. In fact, they hardly think twice about signing on the dotted line when opportunities for reenlistment come around. Working on Don's Christian education staff is a natural, happy way to serve. Dropouts are few and far between.

What is Don's formula? Personality? Friendly persuasiveness? Talent? Skill? Maybe a little of each. But one fact about Don you can't miss is that he appears to be far more interested in people than he is in programs—in *who* people are rather than in *what* they do.

I've observed Don firsthand from time to time; I've talked with people who work for him. One of the things we see Don doing extremely well is making his workers feel valuable. Staff members frequently get handwritten notes from Don on brown monogrammed stationery: "Your story on Moses for the Junior Sunday school department was topnotch—smooth delivery, insightful commentary, and excellent mastery of the material. Congratulations." One note of appreciation like that keeps the engines fueled for a long time. At the end of each church year, Don rents a banquet room in a downtown Holiday Inn, and over candlelight and prime rib he says "thank you" to the people on his staff who make the ministry go. The spotlight falls not on the professional platform people but on the teacher who Sunday after Sunday teaches junior boys in the corner classroom right next to the furnace.

We all shift into high gear when we're praised for what we're already doing well. Apparently Don understands that dynamic about people, and that's one clue as to why his workers keep returning.

There are other clues as well.

It was Sunday morning—right at the time when a Christian education director is supposed to be twenty-five places at once. Don probably had twice that many things on his mind. But three young mothers had something on their minds too—the deplorable condition of the toddler nursery where their children spent Sunday mornings. These mothers stopped Don in the hallway to talk.

Rule number one: Stop walking, turn off the eight-track running full speed in your mind, look the other person directly in the eyes, and listen. Rule number two: Determine the other person's real needs. Rule number three: If criticism is involved, let the other person be a part of your solution. Don did all three. At the end of a very short conversation, Don had breakfast scheduled with the three mothers.

By the end of the breakfast meeting, the four had charted a course of action for the nursery dilemma: an all-expense-paid trip for the concerned mothers to two churches in towns where Don knew successful nursery programs were being run. The investigative team brought back pencil sketches for room designs, lists of equipment needs, ideas for toddler curriculum, and even possibilities for staff.

The nursery renovation plan was off and running. No one had to motivate mothers already energized by a need. An alert leader listened, ferreted out feelings, provided support and resources, and made the mothers part of the solution. Experts in the field of toddler nurseries? Don has convinced them that they are.

Stop by the toddler nursery in churches like Don's on Sunday mornings and you will find efficient, enthusiastic workers who are giving every ounce of extra energy to the program they helped to create.

Why do workers, whether in the church or in industry, withhold emotional involvement from their jobs? Because, says

Daniel Yankelovich, we no longer provide the incentives that motivate people—values and a sense of personal worth.

For those of us who claim allegiance to the Lord who specializes in people, there is no excuse for us not to specialize in people. When all our sophisticated recruitment programs are said and done, we are left with a simple example—the carpenter from Nazareth who saw past the exteriors of people and skillfully and gently moved them toward commitment.

21

Kindling Their Vision

*Motivating with inner vision is an art and
is accomplished as much by what we don't do
as it is by what we do.*

—Wayne Jacobsen

The phone shatters the Monday morning quiet. "Pastor, I'm
sorry to bother you on your day off, but I won't be teaching
my children's class anymore. I know it's only been a month, but
it just hasn't been as much fun as I thought. It's a lot of work,
and I'm sure God has something better for me."

Once again, ministry succumbs to cost.

How often has this happened not only in service but in discipleship as well? I actually had a young lady try to convince
me there was no contradiction between her claim to be a Christian and her promiscuous lifestyle. "With all the sexual temptations of our day, God certainly can't expect a single person to
be celibate."

Who is teaching this crossless gospel—full of fun and glitter
but devoid of personal cost? Not the one who said, "If anyone
would come after me, he must deny himself and take up his
cross daily and follow me" (Luke 9:23).

Pointed words, no doubt, if time has not worn them into
mere poetic abstraction. God has given us great and glorious
promises, but we possess them only as we follow him in the
face of self-denial, not as we frolic in self-satisfaction.

That's the dilemma for pastors—we who must motivate human beings. How do we get people to embrace what costs so much, especially in an age where personal enjoyment is king?

Surprise Them!

In the same way we can make a child eat peas by hiding them in the spoon we just magically turned into an airplane, maybe we can get people to the cross if we sneak it up on them unannounced.

Ignore those distressing Scriptures about dying to self. To meet the needs of our culture, we have to start where people are, and ours are after self-fulfillment and self-esteem. Therefore, we need to focus on God's blessings—forgiveness, freedom, heaven. Downplay what must be surrendered to him—the right to please ourselves.

We can keep a little of the cost, calling people to periodic church attendance, a nominal monetary contribution, and an outwardly good life. People will go that far (after all, any religion worth believing ought to require something), but a cross is archaic.

All would be well, except that to ignore the challenges of discipleship will not bear the test of time. The door to Christ's life is marked "Obedience," and that's not always fun. Christianity without sacrifice eventually turns out as bland as it is unreal. People either get tired of it or disillusioned by it.

And you can't expect them to swallow a hidden cost when it emerges. That's why Jesus said to count the cost before you start.

Pay Them!

"What's the easiest way to motivate people?" I have been asked that question often, and I have no doubts about my answer.

Pay them!

Salaries provide excellent leverage for commitment and accountability. Not that the average Christian can be bought, but
we are all well ingrained with the American work ethic. I've
never heard of a paid staff member calling late on Saturday
night to say he couldn't teach the next morning because Aunt
Maude was throwing a family reunion at eleven-thirty.

Making Christianity the source of someone's bread and but-
ter is a great solution. If you don't believe me, look at ex-pastors
who have taken other avenues of ministry or employment. Ever
notice how those who so eloquently addressed their congregations about tithing or regular attendance have a hard time living up to it when the church no longer signs their checks?

Of course, we cannot afford to put everyone on staff. But
don't despair; other variations on this salary idea can be equally
effective.

"We know that people will give more to this ministry out of
greed than out of a pure heart. Since we're using their money
for godly purposes, we don't mind appealing to greed to get it."
To my great shock, that guideline came from the mouth of the
chief fund-raiser of one of America's well-known Christian ministries. No doubt this is Christian fund-raising at its worst, but
the point is made. There are other things besides money to offer
people in the face of sacrifice. For instance . . .

Special status. "Become a 'partner' in this ministry" or
"We're looking for a Women's Ministry Coordinator, and if your
family wants to make this its church home, I'm sure you'd be
just perfect" or "For a one-thousand-dollar donation, we'll en-
shrine your name in our Hall of Faith."

People will do a lot for status. And according to the fund-
raiser, a lot more for status than because of obedience. People
want to feel important and know that others recognize their efforts. Organs, pulpits, and entire educational wings can be acquired by offering to put the donor's name on them for all to
see.

Acclaim. You can't give everyone a title without eventual
devaluation. So use titles only for special needs that require a

lot of hard work with little reward, and use personal acclaim or affirmation to motivate for smaller needs.

Every person serving in the church ought to get a letter or personal call from the pastor periodically, right? Any good pastor should spend a day a week writing thank-you notes or recruiting. There was a pastor in my city who called one of our elders and asked him and his wife to be leaders in his church because they were such "good people." The possibilities here are limitless.

Freedom from guilt. People will do a lot to alleviate guilt. But for the church to use this adequately, it must first create the guilt so it can provide the way to relief. "After all Jesus has done for us, is a thousand dollars too much to ask to help with our building fund?" "How many souls have you led to Christ over the last year? At the downtown mission, we've touched over five hundred people. Your contributions give you part of the credit for that."

Few Christians live in the security that they are meeting all of God's expectations. Probe the fringes of guilt, and you'll obtain an immediate response. People will do a lot to salve it.

Guilt can be used without people even realizing it. Appeal to a sense of loyalty: "Won't you do this as a special favor to your pastor?" and people think they're motivated by love. Or use crises: "Unless you give today, this ministry will not be able to continue," and their guilt will look like generosity.

Relieved fears. "The fires of hell rage hot. Who knows but that tonight on your way home you'll die in a car accident and get a taste of its flames if you don't volunteer for the nursery?"

That's a bit overdone, I admit, but fear *is* an All-American in the sport of motivation. My greatest year of discipleship as a child came after I thought I'd missed the Rapture. A change of family plans and a missed message brought me home from school by bus when my parents had picked up my other brothers. I was in sixth grade, and as the bus emptied, I noted my brothers were not aboard. Maybe Jesus had come back and I had been left (which, given my lifestyle in the past couple of weeks, was not unthinkable).

I ran the quarter mile to our house and found it empty. Alone for the next hour, I prepared my life to meet the Beast and the Great Tribulation. Eventually the family returned, to my great relief, but in the ensuing months I found it easier to walk in righteousness.

Plain and simple, all of these options work. They've been tried and tested in church programs for years. You can stake your ministry on them.

But I'm not sure you should.

Expediency Problems

I probably should have admitted this earlier, but I wanted you to read this far. I'm not a pragmatist. I care less about what works than what's right. In the long run that's what yields enduring fruit.

People do respond when someone appeases their desire for success or their self-doubt, but have we looked at the long-range implications of motivating people this way? I find four that bother me.

First and foremost, these tactics are a step away from new covenant motivation. They don't rest on inward change and a personal calling to please the Father, but on personal expedience—what's in it for me? Anyone will do an unpleasant task if the compensation matches the cost. Jesus adequately warned us that fear will never work in the long run, and serving him to be seen by others is fruitless activity.

Second, they put the priority on activities, not people. The task is the end; people are only the means. No wonder people eventually wear out. Serving in children's ministries because of guilt wears someone on two fronts—the guilt that lingers and carrying on a task not freely chosen. This approach only works with an ever-expanding base of participants, where the incoming replace the burned-out. Biblical priorities compel us to reject such a notion and realize people are the goal of all ministry.

Third, the pastor turns into a promoter. Some are comfortable with this; I am not. If a pastor feeds and equips his congregation, he shouldn't have to waste time thinking up tactics to keep the sheep cooperative.

Finally, though these methods will get response, they are not ultimately effective. I know I risk sounding like a pragmatist with a statement like that, but there are barriers in personal growth and ministry that expedience will never cross. How do you make "dying to the flesh" worthwhile circumstantially? Following Jesus doesn't always lead to immediate benefits. Our marching orders are clear: "He who wants to save his life must lose it."

There's no way to make expedient the giving up of a night's sleep to counsel someone through a painful bondage into God's freedom, or driving 250 miles to help a single mother move into a new apartment in a strange city, or risking vulnerability with new people after having just been taken advantage of by the last ones. I've seen people do all these with joy, because they were motivated by something deeper than expedience.

Rees Howells, the Welsh coal miner turned intercessor, understood it. His father didn't. During one period of his life, Rees led a Bible study in a distant village. Every night he walked two miles each way to minister—after a twelve-hour day in the mines. One night he came home in the middle of a downpour, completely soaked. "I wouldn't have walked across there tonight for twenty pounds," his father said when he saw him.

"Nor would I for twenty pounds," answered Rees.

People motivated like that don't need a salary, a thank-you plaque, fear, or pressure—and they don't burn out either. Their motivation flows from a deep well of vision within. The responsibility of leadership is to uncap that well.

Inner-Vision Cultivation

Having explored all the options to their bitter end, we still don't have an answer to our question. How do you excite someone about dying on a cross?

You don't.

There's nothing exciting about it. Crosses are endured, not cherished. They are faced not out of rabid excitement but out of personal Gethsemanes where obedience to the Father takes precedence over personal expedience. That's the vision that burns in the heart—to please God and participate in his work regardless of cost.

Paul tapped that inner well. He was not a promoter, selling out the means to whatever noble end he or God had in mind. He avoided "persuasive words" so that faith might not rest on mere "wisdom, but on God's power" (1 Corinthians 2:4–5). We need more people motivated by God's vision growing within, not the stirring appeal of a great orator. The former endures cost; the latter flashes for a moment and then vanishes in a wake of worn-out people.

Motivating with inner vision is an art and is accomplished as much by what we don't do as by what we do.

1. *To inspire without bribing.*

"We have renounced secret and shameful ways; we do not use deception, nor do we distort the word of God. On the contrary, by setting forth the truth plainly we commend ourselves to every man's conscience in the sight of God" (2 Corinthians 4:2–3).

Here Paul is more specific about his method of motivating people. He denies himself the tools we considered earlier and gives us three simple steps.

First, set forth the truth plainly. Ministry goes astray whenever its goal becomes motivation instead of clarity. How often are we tempted to be ambiguous with God's Word for fear it might offend someone? We go to great pains to make Scripture palatable, when our efforts would be better spent making it clear. The Gospel *will* offend people; that's God's responsibility. Making it clear is ours.

Having made the truth plain, Paul then commends it to people's consciences. Let them wrestle with the facts—not guilt, fear, or possible reward by the minister. Don't make the decision for them. What good is it for someone to do for the pastor what that same person wouldn't do for Jesus? He'd be better off if we didn't stir up a flurry of activity to mask that reality.

That's exactly how our congregation handles finances. We've decided not to pass offering plates. A box sits in the back; people leave their gifts there or else mail them to the church office. We do teach God's call to be givers, but we don't want people giving because others are watching or because their guilt mushrooms the nearer the plate comes to their seat.

I'm not saying it's wrong to pass an offering plate or that we never will. But we won't do it simply to get more money. We intend to function on guilt-free dollars. The amount may be less, but it will be what people have chosen to give freely, and we don't have to engage in constant pre-offering hype. Meanwhile, the mere mention of needs outside our fellowship unleashes a spring of generosity.

Finally, Paul says this process goes on under God's watchful eye. The application is twofold. For Paul, that fact kept him dependent on the Lord for his ministry, not people's response. For the Corinthians, they were not to gaze at God's will like a smorgasbord, choosing only what they wanted. Our lives must seek God's pleasure, not our own. For that we are accountable.

Building God-motivated people begins when we stop trying to motivate them and clearly set God's plan before them instead. We must help free them from the bondages of expedience, not use them for our own ends.

2. To direct without manipulating.

Even Paul's guidelines to ministry can become heavy-handed if we're the ones directing people's responses. That's not what Paul meant. His ministry directed people to God, but it didn't direct their ministries. The Holy Spirit is responsible to place members in the body as he sees fit.

He will if we'll equip them. We do that by building in every believer a meaningful relationship with the Father expressed by daily reading and prayer, measured by a growing sensitivity and obedience to his will.

We also equip them by creating an environment of responsibility. Church structures often fail here. People resist responsibility. They simply want to come, enjoy the service, and go home. But if a body is a family and there are duties to be done, they must be shared openly.

At our church, parents don't come regularly without getting involved in child discipleship. We assume they'll share that responsibility unless they tell us otherwise. Every parent who hasn't volunteered to teach or help with crafts in one of our children's classes is rotated into our nursery schedule. Child discipleship is not a *service* provided by our church; it's a *cooperative effort* of our whole body. Leadership, then, focuses on equipping people instead of recruiting them.

This environment is the medium that cultivates inner vision. If the foundation is well laid, there is never a problem in meeting the genuine needs of this fellowship. People understand what God wants of them and move without pastoral intervention.

Recently we had a unique wedding. This couple had earlier been dismissed from our church for persistent sin. They had since repented and been welcomed back into the body. Now they wanted to get married, with two weeks' notice, following one of our Sunday morning services. They didn't have much money, nor did they want to take time to add frills.

Without any encouragement from the pastoral staff, the body went to work. Some people planned a reception—cake, nuts, and everything—to follow the brief ceremony. Someone *made* wedding rings, which the couple couldn't have afforded. Another secured two nights' use of a company condominium and collected enough money to get them there. Others showed up early with flowers and greenery to decorate our rented facility, and someone else loaned the bride a dress.

How could anyone have organized such an affair in so short a time? How inappropriate it would have been for me to ask people to donate rings or a condominium. When I asked people why they pitched in, I kept hearing the same answer: "It's what I felt God wanted me to do."

God-motivated people are God-directed people. How much more powerful when ministry is orchestrated by the Holy Spirit, not the pastor!

3. *To release without hyping.*

If we had a wedding committee in our fellowship to handle situations like the above, we'd regularly have to recruit people to staff it. Programs need hype because they become jobs, not extensions of vision.

Programs are not the basis of ministry—personal relationships are. We put people in high-touch situations so that ministry is not serving a program but loving a person. Any of us will give more to a friend who can't feed her baby than we'll give in an offering for starving children overseas. The first is sacrifice, the second is a donation.

Personal relationships spawn effective ministry. Not a week goes by that I don't hear of someone sharing money, time, transportation, or housing with someone in need, and I'm sure I hear only a fraction of what is really happening. We've taken the same approach to missions. We began to pursue ties with Ethiopia two years before the famine became well known. We've had Ethiopian nationals speak here, we've given offerings for the current crisis, and we're helping resettle four refugees from that country. Eventually we want to found a sister congregation in that or another country.

So when we read about Ethiopia in *Time*, our hearts are on the line. It's personal with us. We're involved. Building relationships with people across the safety lines of cultural barriers transforms ministry into a daily reality.

God-motivated individuals get excited about people, not programs. Helping people build relationships primes the well of inner vision.

Uncontrolled Motivation

Does this kind of visionary motivation work? Truthfully, it does, but not always the way a pastor wants it to. It doesn't make for a streamlined organization where everyone conforms to the latest institutional objective. But it does produce people ready and willing to serve at a moment's notice without regard to personal convenience.

Through a major miscommunication, we found out a ministry team would be coming to our city on only ten days' notice. Could we house thirty young men overnight and have a Friday night service? We agreed to sponsor it jointly with another church five times larger than we are. We'd each house half the ex-drug addicts.

When all was said and done, the other church couldn't find one home. Our people volunteered for all thirty, even though for many families it meant a major change in plans.

"Because I felt that's what God wanted!" was what they said.

Tap that, and you'll find a wealth of people growing in Jesus and ministering for him. You can't always control their efforts, but whatever made us think we were supposed to?

22

Keeping Leaders Aflame

Interpersonal conflict is a primary cause of burnout.

—Robert J. Morgan

J osh was one of the most zealous workers we'd seen at church, but I realized he was three steps beyond "weary in well doing" when I read his letter:

> My walk with the Lord is nonexistent. I've allowed the pressures of church work to crowd out time with God. Now it seems impossible to get back in touch with him. We've also gotten seriously into debt, and I've been trying to do "ministry" while working five part-time jobs. I'm short with my wife and kids, and we're having problems. I'd like to talk to you. . . .

To keep volunteers from stagnation, frustration, and burnout, I'm learning from several pages in the "Operations Manual."

Ezekiel: Think Empathetically

A friend dropped out of pastoring for a while, taking a "normal" job. He later told me, "I have new respect for laypeople. I can't possibly do everything I once asked of my workers."

I've thought a lot about his words. He was learning, like Ezekiel, to sit where they sat (Ezekiel 3:15). When we do, we gain respect for people's schedules, and we guard workers against overinvolvement.

Last night, I grew wary while chatting with a new member, a hard-driving sales executive thrilled with his new Christian life and eager to be involved.

"I've signed up for drama ministry," he told me. "We practice on Wednesdays. I have Bible study on Thursday nights and church softball on Fridays. We're going to a Sunday school function on Saturday."

"I don't expect you to be here every night of the week," I said.

As far as I'm concerned, the unwritten motto of lay ministry should be: One Person, One Ministry. That may be unrealistic, but it gives us a goal and keeps us sensitive to demands on our workers.

Nehemiah: Create Systems

Years ago, Jim, who was in charge of our buildings and grounds, planned a church workday. Several dozen people sacrificed extra sleep for thankless toil. But I was disappointed to find that Jim hadn't organized the activities. A hallway needed painting; there were no paint cans, brushes, or drop cloths. Floors needed mopping; one old mop and pail occupied the janitor's closet. Most of us stood around trying to look busy, thoroughly frustrated. And only two people showed up for the next workday—so I was told.

Nehemiah went about it differently. He created systems. The projected wall was divided into manageable sections with clearly defined tasks. Some were stationed as watchmen, others as soldiers. Others provided food. Workers hauled off debris as it accumulated. Everyone understood his or her part, and the wall went up.

Local churches are difficult places to create efficient systems, for they are volunteer organizations made up of people with varying levels of ability, maturity, and dedication. Several things have helped us create or maintain systems.

Periodic retreats with staff or layleaders are worth every penny. We get away to the mountains semiannually to look at our church ministries. We ask, "What systems must be in place, working effectively, to accomplish together what God wants us to do?" We develop organizational charts (a simpler task than it sounds, thanks to computer software).

Recently, our staff met in Cincinnati to take in a Reds' game and to isolate ourselves for two days of evaluation and planning. While away, we learned that the wife of our oldest member had fallen ill. By long-distance, we referred the need to the man's Sunday school class with its teacher, laypastor, and tight circle of friendships. I was upset to learn later that no one called, visited, prepared food, or prayed with the family.

We treated it as a systems failure—"Houston, we have a problem." We met with class leaders to find out where the caring process broke down. We were careful not to be critical, but concerned. Everyone now understands the processes better, and I don't expect a recurring problem.

It takes longer to solve problems on a systems level. It's demanding to both minister and administer. But somewhere near or at the top of a productive, motivated organization is a Nehemiah.

Syzygus: Reduce Friction

During an intense capital stewardship campaign, two of our workers argued over decorations for the celebration supper. Claude had acquired three hundred pine seedlings, thinking they could be potted in cups and placed at each dinner setting. "People can plant their pines as symbols of our growth," he said. "They'll always be reminded, seeing their trees, of this period in our church's life."

It was a good idea, but it didn't suit the decorations planned by Anne, who visualized fine china and tasteful elegance—not pine trees and potting soil. They had a terrible row, and I hurried over to Claude's house, where his wife met me at the car, wringing her hands. "Have you come to help us with our problem?" she asked. I nodded grimly and went inside. When Claude told me his side of the story, I sensed he'd lost his temper and spoken harshly to Anne.

"Claude," I said, "you've got to visit her and apologize."

"I did!" he said. "I did apologize. It didn't do any good."

"What did you say?" I asked.

"I told her I was sorry."

"You did?"

"Yes," he said, voice rising. "I told her I was sorry she was acting so immaturely."

It took all my powers of diplomacy to patch things up (we finally stuck the trees in elegant little flowerpots and handed them out as people left the ballroom), but both families eventually left the church.

Interpersonal conflict is a primary cause of burnout, so we take on the role of the loyal yokefellow in Philippians 4:2–3: "I urge Euodia and Syntyche to iron out their differences and make up. . . . Syzygus, since you're right there to help them work things out, do your best with them" (The Message).

So we strive to mediate or prevent conflict. We're arranging lunch with a member of our missions team who has been unusually silent during the last few meetings—or absent altogether. I think she's upset, and I'd like to talk with her.

Syzygus would have.

Paul: Give Recognition

Ever heard of Urbanus, Apelles, Tryphena, and Tryphosa? They weren't the most famous New Testament servants, but they must have beamed when the apostle Paul mentioned their hard work in Romans 16. Paul's example prompted us to create opportunities like these:

• Showing slides during the prelude or offertory on selected

Sundays, highlighting workers in various areas of church life.

- Implementing an annual Lay Ministry Sunday with videos, testimonies, sermons, and sometimes a staff-hosted dinner for recognizing faithful workers.
- Showing videos of special events. Following our annual Kids' Jamboree, for example, we show two videos on successive Sundays—one featuring the kids, the other highlighting our workers.
- Presenting profiles in our church newsletter.
- Utilizing notes, calls, words of love, and lots of hugs from staff and members.
- Appointing an annual Lay Minister of the Year. This year's recipient was director of our teen choir. When Missy came forward to receive her plaque, teens from all over the audience rose spontaneously, joined her, and sang their theme to her, "Heaven Is Counting on You."

We can't do these things every week, but we consistently monitor and nurture morale. This means becoming Ezekiels and Nehemiahs and taking cues from Syzygus and Paul. This means work.

But nothing works without it.

23

The Manipulation Game

I cannot allow the fear of manipulation
to be a rationalization for not doing
the hard work of instilling motivation.

—Fred Smith, Sr.

I recently heard a pastor tell about a wealthy oil man who called and said, "Reverend, I've never had much time for religion, but I'm getting older, and maybe I ought to make my peace with the church. I'd like to start by giving you a $20,000 check."

The preacher said, "I immediately extended to him the right hand of Christian fellowship."

I don't think he was joking.

The exchange was an example of manipulation, which despite being repudiated still manages to find its way into the ministry.

Manipulation is often used because it's effective—it just plain works! In this case, the church got a $20,000 windfall. But manipulation comes with a price. The pastor manipulated the fellow into believing he was getting Christian fellowship, but the man also manipulated the preacher by buying his way in, and that, as we all know, is no real relationship at all.

In contrast, a young man named Philip makes films with Christian themes. He became acquainted with a non-Christian who shared his interest in film-making techniques but rejected the importance of personal commitment to Christ.

The non-Christian offered some valuable equipment, and Philip said gently, "I appreciate the offer, but I can't accept the equipment unless you fully recognize that this gift does not get you any points with God. Your eternal destination is determined by your relationship with Christ, not whether you contribute to Christian films. Do you understand that?"

"I understand," the friend said.

"Then I'll accept the equipment."

Those two stories illustrate the difference between manipulation and motivation. Motivation is getting people to do something out of mutual advantage. Manipulation is getting people to do what you want them to do, primarily for *your* advantage. With manipulation, if the other person benefits, it's purely secondary.

Manipulation carries a hidden agenda. Motivation carries an open agenda. You can be totally honest with people.

The young film maker was saying, "Do we have enough mutual interest to get all the agenda on top of the table? I'm not going to manipulate you or let you manipulate me into a brownie-point religion."

Which Is It?

We all agree that motivation is good and manipulation is bad. But sometimes only a fine line separates the two, and it's difficult to know which side of the line you're on. The issues aren't always clear-cut—what may be a legitimate case of motivation in one situation could, with a different intent, be manipulation.

An example is a cook who hides eggplant, which you've said you'll never eat, in a casserole. You say, "Hey, that's good. What is it?" Only then does he tell you. Were you manipulated? Or motivated?

A psychiatrist friend chided me one night by saying, "You businessmen mistake manipulation for motivation. The difference is you can substitute the word *thirst* for motivation but not manipulation." He was saying unless you are satisfying someone's thirst, you are probably manipulating rather than motivating. I've found this to be a good principle for distinguishing the two. I can motivate with integrity when I am bringing to consciousness a genuine thirst.

I was motivated in my appreciation of Dixieland music, for instance, by former Senator S. I. Hayakawa. He was an absolute authority on Dixieland, and we spent a pleasant evening discussing it. Later I realized that he, an excellent teacher and semanticist, had instilled a deeper interest than I'd had before.

He said, for example, "Cool jazz is courteous. Dixieland is discourteous because everybody talks at the same time. At the end of a number, after everybody's made a statement and they 'take it home,' everyone starts making a statement at the same time." He played on my intellectual interest to attract me to Dixieland.

He never said, "I'm going to try to intrigue you." He simply intrigued me.

Was that manipulation? I don't think so because I already had some interest and he merely deepened it. Now I can listen to a band and tell which musicians are really making statements and which are just putting in time.

Whenever we try to motivate without the other person knowing what we are trying to do, however, we need to be careful. We can try to bring out a latent desire a person doesn't even know exists, but we need to remember to do three things: (1) Recognize how close we are to manipulation, (2) set a checkpoint, and if the technique doesn't produce a genuine thirst, stop it, and (3) never resort to immoral means even for righteous ends.

A friend had a secretary who lived an uninhibited life-style with no apparent interest in the Christian way. One day a letter arrived for him from a student named Ed who closed with "Until I hear from you, I'll be floating around." My friend wrote him back, basically explaining how he could find spiritual reality without floating around. He rewrote that letter half a dozen times, not because he was dissatisfied with what he said the first time, but so it would have to be retyped by the secretary, who also was "floating around."

In a sense, that bordered on manipulation. But I feel (others may differ) that it was done with integrity. Because my friend admitted to himself what he was doing, he ended it after a limited time; and his action did not exploit the woman—he was paying her a full salary for the typing.

Later he found she kept a copy of the letter for herself, and she eventually became a Christian. The process started with her typing that letter to Ed.

Instilling motivation is hard work. It takes a lot out of me to bring you where I want you to go. I sometimes hear people say, "Well, if a person doesn't want to go, I have no right to manipulate him to get him there." I may not have a right to manipulate, but neither can I allow the fear of manipulation to be a rationalization for not doing the hard work of instilling motivation, which is, after all, one of the leader's most important tasks.

At the same time, we limit anything that borders on manipulation because it is so easy to exploit people with it. To challenge people, to motivate with integrity, means I may put a lot of effort into a person, but the time comes when he must be set free. He may walk away and leave me empty-handed, but any more on my part would be dishonest manipulation. My only recourse is to start over with somebody else.

I once recommended to a young woman a particular church because she wanted to meet some sharp professional people. I sensed, however, that she wasn't very interested in spiritual things, so I didn't keep encouraging her to go. She would not have been going for the right reason.

I simply wanted her to be exposed to the spiritual to see if there was any interest, to give the Spirit of God a chance to work. In this case, apparently the time wasn't right, so I felt any more pushing would have been manipulation.

Uses and Abuses

In most cases, manipulation is the prostitution of motivation. Prostitution is always easier than the real thing; it's an attempt to get results without honest investment. Motivation is not a quick fix; manipulation can be.

A common example in the church is prooftexting, where someone takes a promise people find very attractive (God wants you in a Rolls Royce) and digs up three or four Bible verses that say God will supply your deepest desire. That's manipulation, not honest instruction.

There are other ways we see manipulation in the church.

Appealing to human gratification

Anything that appeals primarily to human desire is manipulation; anything that satisfies divine desires is motivation.

If we structure a church so members come only to meet their human needs for friendship, security, belonging, or tradition, we are manipulating.

To find ways to motivate spiritually is difficult. It's much easier to find a human mutual interest than to implant a divine mutual interest. Divine interests may contradict human interests. If you decide church officers must fulfill the scriptural requirements for deacon or elder, think of the political fallout! In many cases, if you don't let the financially powerful exert their influence, they go to another church, or worse, wreak havoc in this one. So we manipulate by giving them human satisfactions: prestige, power, and authority in the congregation.

Flimsy assurances

Sometimes we satisfy people too easily—with meetings. One Christian woman I know quit attending missionary society meetings because she said they didn't do anything but meet, eat, and have a short prayer. The worst part, she said, was that everyone left feeling they had done something for missions when in fact they'd done nothing. The activity was manipulative—getting people to think they were working when they were actually only keeping busy.

Relying on recognition

I once talked with a young man who planned to give a large donation to establish a Christian institution.

"Are you doing this because God needs it?" I asked.

"Yes, I think so," he said.

"Are you going to put your name on it?"

"Yes, I'd planned to."

"Then I don't think you're spiritually mature enough to do it," I said.

He had the honesty to say, "That may be true. Maybe I'd better think about it for a while." Several years later, he dropped the idea because his motivations have matured.

Selective appreciation

When a wealthy person gives a gift larger than other people but small compared to what he is capable of giving, exaggerated recognition for that gift is manipulative. It does not motivate.

Occasionally I see people recognized as outstanding leaders when the only outstanding thing they've done is give more money than other people can afford. It hasn't affected their lives; it represented no sacrifice. Fawning over them is favoritism, which is condemned in Scripture.

Misuse of "ministry"

I saw an ad on a seminary bulletin board for a secretarial job opening. It listed the normal skills required and then said, "Pay is low because it is a ministry." I wanted to tear it down.

I haven't the vaguest idea why a secretary working in a "Christian" setting should make less than a secretary in a "secular" setting. I understand even less how the location determines whether the secretary's job is a ministry.

I wouldn't mind if the ad had said, "We pay according to

how much support we receive" or "Pay depends on how well the organization does financially." But to spiritualize low wages as "ministry" is manipulation.

These forms of manipulation are usually justified because they help the cause. But in the work of God, ends—even noble ends—never justify means. Such thinking humanizes God and eliminates his sovereignty. God becomes unnecessary as we presume to do for him what he couldn't do in any other way. We forget God is as interested in the process by which we live as the product we produce. If that process is not divinely sanctioned, we are outside his will.

Means of Motivating

What are some motivational means? How can we bring out the best in people without resorting to manipulative tactics?

Establish a tangibly friendly atmosphere

This is especially true with co-workers, whether volunteer or paid. In the corporate world, for instance, I'm very straightforward when hiring: I prefer "my kind of people"—people I can motivate. I can't motivate everybody. It's easier to manipulate than motivate. For long-term, day-to-day relationships, however, I need people I can motivate with integrity. I have never been able to fully motivate somebody I didn't like.

But when I've genuinely motivated someone, I can look him or her in the eye and know we have an honest, friendly relationship between us.

Enjoy people's uniqueness

Being friends is beneficial; having the same tastes is not necessary.

One young woman worked for me matching colors of ink. She could get tears in her eyes over certain shades of blue. "Isn't this a beautiful match?" she'd ask.

I never could figure what went on in her head to make

matching blues such a remarkable occurrence. But all I needed to do to keep her motivated was to share her excitement and appreciate her work.

Know a person's capabilities

With this employee, the most unkind thing I could have done would have been to say, "Don't you think of anything more important than shades of blue?" The truth of the matter was, more often than not, she didn't. Nor would my criticism have made her a better person. She was helping the company by doing what she enjoyed.

I must spend time to know what a person can do. My responsibility is to make as objective an evaluation as I can of present skills, potential capacities, level of commitment, ability to be motivated, discipline, and intensity. If I am to lead, I owe it to my people to take the time to evaluate them well.

The key is not to let feelings override judgment. I try to be as objective with a person as I am with money. If I count your money, the fact that I like you won't make me adjust the bottom line. I need to be just as objective about ability, drive, and dedication.

My color matcher didn't have extensive capabilities, and to motivate her above her capacity would have been cruel. If a musician has limited talent, it's a sin to talk about the joys of being a Mozart. When you're with a woman who is single at age fifty-five, you don't overdo motherhood. In motivation, desire must be matched with ability. You focus on the advantages of being who you are and not what somebody else is.

Motivation always looks to the future.

Know how much responsibility a person can take

Some people can take sizable responsibility but not sole responsibility. They may have great abilities, but something in their psyche says, *I don't want the whole load. I want somebody to lean on, to report to.*

Some people work best with assignments rather than responsibility. Assignments mean you explain what you want, when you want it, and how you want it done. Responsibility means the person takes initiative and gets the job done effectively by whatever means he or she develops.

Good leaders know which kind of people are working for them.

Look for ways both of you can benefit

A certain honesty is required in motivation. It admits that unless there is a mutual interest, perhaps we shouldn't get involved in this thing together.

If a person does have potential, a good question to ask is: "You have a lot more talent than you've been able to put to use. How much effort are you willing to exert if we give you the opportunity to develop that talent?"

The development, of course, has to be in line with the ministry. I wouldn't invest church resources to train somebody who wanted to be a watchmaker. We have to find the mutual advantage. But we can be looking for individuals who want to develop certain skills from which the church can benefit. When a person sees he or she is improving in some area, and it is also helping the body, this is a powerful motivation.

Be honest about your goals

A young minister came to see me not long ago. He wanted to know how he could build his small church into a big church.

"What's your primary motivation?" I asked.

"Frankly, the size church I've got can't pay me enough to live on," he said.

For him to begin an evangelism program, he would have to manipulate people. He couldn't be honest about it.

His church was big enough to support a pastor if he could convince them to tithe, but he'd rather go into a church expansion program than try to teach people to tithe.

Use people as positive illustrations

In my speaking, I've told how certain people excelled at something, perhaps a Christian virtue, and they seemed to love being mentioned that way and consequently began to exhibit even more of those positive traits. This becomes manipulation only if what you're saying is untrue or slanted—or if you threaten to use a person as a bad illustration.

One of the ways I motivate people to think is to always carry some blank cards in my pocket, and when anyone says something worth writing down, I do so. For years I tried to remember memorable lines until I was alone and could jot myself a note. Then I overheard someone say, "I didn't know it was that good, but he wrote it down!" I realized people love to be quoted. And quoting them motivates them to think better.

Now in conversation I'll often say, "May I write that down?" It has excellent motivating power.

One of the nicest compliments you can earn is "He makes me think smart when I'm with him." It's a sign you are motivating people to think.

Give a person a reputation to uphold

One of my bosses had a way of saying nice things about his workers that got back to them. True things but nice things. We appreciated it, and we couldn't keep from trying to do more things he could tell about. People will work hard to uphold a good reputation.

Ask, *What is special about this person?* For example, some people rarely say anything negative. That's a beautiful reputation to start giving them. "Here's a person who looks for the best in others." Of course, you can't be dishonest and say that about a cynic.

I have consciously augmented my wife's reputation as a creative listener. She is. I did it basically to comfort her because she'd always say after a social occasion, "I didn't have anything to say. All I did was listen." And yet she does that better than anyone I know.

One night at a dinner party, she was sitting next to a quiet, powerful man. His wife, sitting next to me, said, "I feel sorry for your wife having to sit next to Jack."

"Jack will talk his head off," I said.

"But you don't know Jack."

"No," I replied, "but I know my wife."

Jack talked his head off. I'm sure his wife thought, *What in the world happened to Jack?* It was simple—Mary Alice has the ability to listen dynamically, to make people feel they're smart. And often they live up to it!

Compliment with credibility

I learned a secret of complimenting from Sarah Jarman, a gracious, intelligent, impeccable woman. Hers were never general compliments, but always specific. "That tie and that suit are exactly right for each other." From then on, I'd wear that tie with that suit.

It was obvious her observations were well thought out, believable, and correct. She never tried to compliment you on something outside her field of expertise. She understood social graces, and the thing she knew best she would compliment you on. She was believable.

I never will forget talking with a professional singer after a concert, and a lady came up and gushed, "You sure did sing well."

The singer thanked her, but after she left, he said, "I could spit."

"Why?" I asked.

"That woman doesn't know how poorly or how well I sang. All she knows is whether or not I made her feel good. I know she meant well, but I wish she'd just said, 'I enjoyed your singing,' rather than rendering a judgment on something she knows little about."

Compliments mean the most when you know what you're talking about.

Show people you enjoy your work

I learned from my former boss, Maxey Jarman, that it was fun to work.

One time, half complaining and half fishing for praise, I said, "I sure am working hard."

Maxey replied, "What would you rather be doing?"

"Oh, nothing else," I had to admit.

"Then," Maxey said matter-of-factly, "you shouldn't complain about doing what you'd rather do."

By observing him and seeing how grateful he was for his responsibility, I realized I liked to work. That's when I had the most fun and satisfaction.

A friend once said, "I was a sophomore at Princeton before I realized it was fun to learn. Then school became exciting." He was fortunate. That doesn't happen to a lot of students until it's too late.

I don't have a higher education, but one of the blessings is that I never learned to study for grades. My friends in higher education have confirmed that those who learned to study for grades are often delayed as thinkers. They say the B students in seminary will often be the best pastors.

Then, tongue in cheek, they say the A students come back as professors and administrators—and they usually wind up calling on the C students for money because they've become the money-makers.

Finding Thirsty People

If the difference between motivation and manipulation is the quenching of thirst, then the key for a leader is to look for thirsty people.

People, however, have different thirsts, and motivating them means knowing what they are thirsty for. Viktor Frankl has taught us that almost everyone has a basic thirst for meaning in life. There are other thirsts: worthwhile accomplishment, utilization of talents, approval by God. One of the greatest for those in Christian work is a thirst to belong, a desire for community in the kingdom of God.

One of the secrets of identifying a person's thirst is to see what has motivated him or her in the past. People rarely outlive their basic thirst. If they get a thirst early in life, they seldom lose it. If they have a thirst for recognition, these people never seem to get quite enough fame. If they thirst for intellectual growth, they never get quite smart enough. If they want money, I rarely see them get to the point where they don't want more.

Then, once we've identified where people are dry, effective motivators ask themselves, *What kind of water do I have to satisfy that kind of thirst?*

When we are able to honestly and openly offer water to parched people, we are not manipulating. We are motivating.

Part 6

Congregational

24

The Idea Behind Motivation

You can't build a head of steam for a weak idea.

—John Cheydleur

L ord, is having a staff a blessing? Or is it just a giant albatross around my neck? Should I fire them all?

In the early '70s, I sat alone one night in a diner in East Orange, New Jersey, and prayed those silent but seeking questions. The staff of our combined church/community center had grown from three to twelve in just over two years, and I was now responsible for a whole new area of ministry—motivating and managing a staff.

While it seemed that God needed all of these people for our ministry, they were a drain on me—a drain on my time, my emotions, my life. I didn't feel qualified to be responsible for so many lives. Besides, my personal ministry seemed to be suffering in direct proportion to the amount of time I was spending in "caretaking" the staff members.

Gary, for example, was a good coordinator, a compassionate assistant pastor, and a wise counselor beyond his years. However, among other momentum-stopping irritations, he usually picked the time right after the Sunday morning services to involve me in complex questions about the politics and procedures of the church. It was the very moment when I needed to be giving my attention to members of the congregation I hadn't seen during the week. It seemed to me, in light of Gary's obvious abilities, that he should help me to reach out to individual members of the church rather than "bug me" about philosophical and organizational matters at an inappropriate time.

God answered my prayer. I found myself being introduced to pastors of larger churches who faced similar problems and were interested in helping me. Management books jumped out at me as I stood in front of bookshelves. Though I viewed certain motivational and management techniques with a disdainful eye, I began an earnest search for principles that were consistent with Scripture.

Incidentally, the sensation of being overwhelmed is one of Satan's favorite ploys to obscure the fact that we are effectively ministering. In my opinion, the old adage "Common sense isn't so common" doesn't apply to the vast majority of Christian leaders. But many of us approach the increasing complexities of ministry with feelings of inadequacy. We've succumbed to a cultural and educational philosophy which teaches that only the highly trained specialist can deal with complicated problems.

For example, my own sense of being overwhelmed prevented me from grasping something vital—that our intense desire to bring Jesus Christ to the people at the bottom rung of society's ladder was a highly focused ministry concept around which God had gathered a very capable staff. Their commitment to this concept motivated them to be deeply involved, even though it often required that they make extreme personal and financial sacrifices. I later learned that one of the most powerful motivational factors in any multi-staff ministry is unified commitment to the same concept of ministry.

Another thing I was doing right (more right than I realized) was meeting with a senior staff member every day. We spent many good times over a cup of coffee discussing ministry ideas that, in turn, expressed my concepts and commitments to her. As our ministry expanded, she always "stood in my corner" even when other people misunderstood or criticized. Because I had taken the time to clearly spell out my ideas and allow a friend to test the strength of them, we built a relationship of confidence, trust, and cooperation. Even when it became necessary for me to help reorganize her department, I received her full cooperation and support because my ideas had been shared, accepted, and tested with her.

Common sense goes a long way toward solving any ministry problem, no matter how large it may seem. Of course, the first rule of common sense is to know when you're in over your head. As Proverbs 11:14 says, "In the multitude of counselors there is safety" (KJV).

While it was reassuring to discover I was doing many right things, it was even more valuable to deliberately probe into the dynamics of motivation.

Seminary professors often tell budding preachers that the strength of a sermon idea can be tested by reducing it to a single sentence. That goes for writers as well. Thus, when trying to define motivation, I would say, "Motivation is the art of taking a strong, vital idea and communicating it in such a way that another person will make it his own and implement it."

Obviously, that's the positive and more formal way of saying it. The flipside is, "You can't build a head of steam for a poorly presented, weak idea."

Both statements point to the heart of motivation—the strength and vitality of an idea. Ideas are the bedrock of motivational dynamics.

A well-known pastor has built a national ministry upon "powerful ideas." To this day, he refuses to consider any ministry concept unless it "is a great thing for God" and "will help hurting people." While his ministry practice clearly demonstrates that he believes there is more to motivation than strong ideas, he has zeroed in on what I believe is the cornerstone of motivation.

How strong are your ministry concepts? Do you assume that because an idea worked last year you can crank it up again this year? Were your ideas that strong last year? Few institutions are more guilty of pushing tired concepts from one year to the next than the church—and we wonder why people never get turned on and involved. A question like, "Oh my goodness, next Sunday is Mother's Day; what are we going to do?" is usually followed by, "Will someone look up the last Mother's Day bulletin and see what we did?"

I believe ministry ideas should be able to pass four tests. While the following tests might seem quite simple on the surface, I have found it's difficult to spell out a ministry concept that will pass all four. However, my own experience plus the experience of many Christian leaders verifies that any worthy ministry concept must pass these tests to sustain motivation.

1. *Ministry concepts must clearly define needs and the specific groups of people who have those needs.*

Sounds pretty basic, doesn't it? Almost simplistic. But how many Christian leaders and/or staff members strive to do everything and serve everybody—somehow? (So that they never serve *anybody* well!) The Institute of Church Growth in Pasadena, California, has clearly documented the value of this test. Its research shows that the most positive forms of church growth usually come from clearly defined concepts of ministry directed toward grouping within the church as well as the community.

When we opened our ministry to the youth of East Orange, New Jersey, it was almost an immediate success. Christine Baldwin, our first director, had a clear ministry idea for the teen center. Christine reminded us that Jesus Christ came to save sinners, not Christians. More specifically, our teen center was to minister to a group of young people who did not want to run the streets with dope pushers, yet were uncomfortable in a traditional church setting. What happened? In addition to attracting and developing a strong staff, our center (three hundred members) produced new converts almost every week. Many of these new Christians eventually moved to positions of leadership in the very churches in which they had not felt comfortable.

2. *Focused ministry concepts succeed; diffused ideas fail.*

Concentrated impact succeeds as well as motivates, for when success occurs, so does self-affirmation. Whatever the measurement, staff members (paid and volunteer) tend to be successful in direct proportion to the focus of their efforts.

This idea has been extrapolated to affect an entire congregation. A friend took me to visit a church in northern New Jersey. As we drove farther and farther into smaller and smaller country lanes, I wondered if there were any buildings up ahead at all, much less a church. Suddenly we emerged upon a thousand-car parking lot surrounding a small, wood-frame building that might have been able to seat 200 persons; across the lane was a larger concrete-block building that might have held 500; and behind it stood a much larger structure that could have held 800 or 900. Adjoining these buildings was a new red-brick "chapel" with white trim that seated 1,300 on the ground floor and 800 in the balcony (full for three Sunday worship services). All of this growth had taken place in five years.

When I asked the pastor to share the story of such accelerated growth, I was prepared for the normal dialogue about goals, master plans, building committees, stewardship campaigns, blueprints, and construction details. Instead, he told me he had spent only one hour in the planning, financing, and construction process. That one hour was spent with the building committee to show them where he would like to place his overhead projector. His ministry concept focused on Bible teaching. Every week he spent over twenty-five hours preparing lessons on overhead transparencies that could be used to teach the Scriptures. Most of his congregation were new converts who carried notebooks as well as Bibles to church.

While I am not suggesting that this ministry idea will produce similar growth for other churches, the principle of focus cannot be denied. Focus builds concentration; concentration builds strength; strength produces successful results; successful results produce new ideas. Ideas must be focused! And all of this comes under the heading of motivation.

3. Ministry concepts must lead to "action conclusions."

An idea that doesn't lead to implementation or decision, regardless of how well defined and focused it is, will result in ministry breakdown and an unmotivated, nonproductive, fizzled-out staff. These symptoms can be found in staff members who skip meetings (or come late), obviously appear bored, and become uncooperative with new ministry ideas.

The ultimate example of this came to my attention while conducting a workshop in staff supervision at the National Association of Christians in Social Work. One harried mission executive wrote a plea for help that said, "My problem is more basic than the things you are talking about; I can't get my staff members to meet together for one hour a week about anything!"

Ministry concepts that lead to action conclusions stand out in sharp relief from all other possibilities. What is an action conclusion? How does it develop from a ministry idea?

In the summer of 1979, the San Diego Evangelical Association was faced with a problem. Its director, the Reverend Ivan Sisk, felt led to resign from his position and resume his former ministry as an evangelist. The board of the association invited me to join them in rethinking their major ministry concepts. Through careful reexamination, the board determined that God was leading them, as individual members, to be involved more personally in the ministries and activities of the organization. What was the action conclusion? A director was hired whose principal skill was in the area of management coordination rather than in public speaking, evangelism, and public relations. Those ministries were now to be functions of the board members. Because they moved through the process of definition, focus, and action conclusion, the board implemented a search for a new director and eventually found a capable pastor who had a background of management in the aerospace industry.

This same process works just as effectively with ministries such as worship, Christian education, discipleship, pastoral care, and interpersonal relations. In fact, one of the most exciting things about exploring definition and focus is that it spontaneously spawns action conclusions. And it's at this point of creative spontaneity that staff members begin to buy into the ministry idea and internalize it as though it were their own. Tune up your ministry ideas in terms of this third test, and watch staff motivation climb!

4. *Ministry concepts must describe the future and how to get there.*

All of us, whether leaders or followers, want to know how the "now" and the "then" are tied together. Participatory planning makes this possible. Nehemiah demonstrated this when he and his staff reconstructed the wall of Jerusalem. He began with a carefully developed plan and specific sessions of participatory planning (2:18). *Here's where we are going* generates maximum power for any ministry idea. Ask the following questions:

A. What is this ministry right now?

B. What should this ministry be in the future?

C. What will have to change for this ministry to become what it should be?

If your ministry idea describes only the present—"We are a 600-member Methodist church on the corner of Fourth and Main"—you probably have a static condition. If your ministry idea suggests, "Our church should expand by ten percent each year to match the population growth of our community," a ministry idea has been planted that may live or may die.

But if your ministry idea declares, "During the next three years our church will grow by 180 members from people who live within a five-mile radius of our sanctuary" or "We will establish a lay-led ministry to the 600 residents of the Parkview retirement community," you've laid a foundation for motivation and momentum on which you can build an exciting outreach program.

These same three questions can be asked of a special occasion like Mother's Day:

A. How are we ministering to our mothers?

B. How should we be ministering to them in the future?

C. What must change to make this happen? And how can a special Mother's Day service contribute to that change?

I have found that successful church staff who have never heard of these four tests still tend to think along these lines. While they might not be conscious of structural dynamics, they are building on strong ideas that have become their own and are being clearly communicated to others. Conversely, churches and organizations that don't think in these terms—in spite of quotas, targets, systems, reporting forms, boxes to fill in, numbers to post—are not growing. Nor are they known for having motivated people in their ranks.

Fortunately, I learned the ideas behind motivation, and as I did, my staff in East Orange, New Jersey, became a tremendous blessing to me. They didn't need me to follow them around and re-motivate them every week. My albatross was gone, but motivated ministry remained.

25

What Lights the Fire

A sense of duty isn't enough for long-haul motivation;
a sense of purpose is.

—Roger Thompson

I t was going to be great! A youth trip with a purpose. Out of
our group of twenty-five high schoolers, twenty-two had
signed up for seven days of nothing but service and discipleship. We were serious: eight hours of work each day, plus Scripture memory and Bible study.

We had talked up, psyched up, and signed up every available body. *That's what comes from good teaching, strategizing,
and planning*, I told myself. And the kids were even paying
their own way!

The final week arrived. As I made call after call, the excuses
mounted. Heavy pencil lines ran through all the leaders' names
. . . and most of the followers. I was reduced to begging. Instead
of an impressive caravan of youth missionaries, we piled into
one station wagon: four silent "fringe" teenagers, two sponsors,
and myself. I was into Round One of an expensive lesson in
leadership and motivation. I was angry and befuddled.

Motivation's Mystery

Motivation is a suspect enterprise, a pseudo-science. It is
loved or hated. Creating and maintaining motivation among

God's people is variously viewed as carnal mass manipulation, flim-flam fund-raising, or somewhere between B. F. Skinner and the black arts.

But motivation is an unavoidable part of any people ministry. Avoidance, fear, or ignorance of the motivational dynamics in a congregation is disastrous both occupationally and spiritually.

I've known churches on both extremes in their views of motivation, and either polarity eventually freezes spiritual health.

One extreme is the bigger-and-better Siss-Boom-Bah hype. "We can do it if we each do our part!" Its stock-in-trade is contagious enthusiasm, colorful charts or graphs or thermometers, achievable goals, and constant reinforcement. Every program is launched by means of visible reward. Numbers are important. Busyness abounds. But what happens when the tents are folded and the ringmaster packs away the megaphone?

No wonder church members who have seen eight pastors come and go are skeptical and tired when we drag out the latest incentives. Often these faithful attenders have never felt valued, trusted, or worthwhile. They are always expected to jump—just like they did thirty years ago—when the pastor says, "Here's the plan." Many who are labeled "burned out" simply want to be treated as grown-ups.

The other extreme for supposed spiritual giants is the disdain-of-anything-tangible school. This approach implies we shouldn't have to work at motivating people. It is beneath the dignity of mature Christians to publicize, thank, or reinforce. All truly spiritual motivation is invisible, intrinsic, mysteriously implanted all at once by God at the time of one's conversion. This sense of duty fuels the loftiest motives of life. No pit stops allowed. We simply call upon that sense of "oughtness" whenever a job needs to be done.

A sell-out to either of these extremes eventually results in anemic, reluctant compliance by a congregation. Absent is the joy of serving, the want-to motivation so necessary for long-term effectiveness.

While the success sellers like Zig Ziglar have turned motivation into a major new service industry, few churches are able to heavily invest in that movement. Nor are they inclined to. Many churches and Christian leaders have discovered a much less expensive incentive: guilt.

Guilt Gets 'Em Going (for a While)

Many of us, wittingly or not, expect a lot from guilt. It is the leverage we use to prop up a sagging budget, enlist volunteers for the nursery, or get movement down the aisles.

Guilt often becomes the pastor's closest and most effective associate. When it comes to getting people moving, it just plain works! And after all, we might ask, why shouldn't people feel guilty for not participating? Not giving? Not serving?

But things are not always as they seem. Guilt, in fact, is a lousy motivator, effective only in the short run. It is a merciless taskmaster and a joyless mentor. Guilt is an impetus with diminishing returns. It is a major cause of the musical-chairs memberships being exchanged in many metropolitan churches.

Chuck, for instance, was a skilled technician who installed the new sound system in his church, ran the tape ministry, sang in the choir, and repaired the organ. As a new Christian, he felt constrained to do whatever the pastoral staff asked of him. The pressing needs and his overactive conscience always kept him overcommitted. After two years of four-nights-a-week service, however, he finally gave up. Quit completely. He went off seeking a church where he could find some rest.

When that happens, something basic is missing. What is worse, a counterfeit has passed for the truth.

All of us, of course, must deal with real guilt. Sin and sloth, when exposed by the piercing ministry of the Holy Spirit, place us guilty before God. It is with God we must deal, for he has convicted us. But real guilt is a warning light, a corrective leading to repentance and forgiveness. It is not meant to fuel the Christian enterprise.

When people run on guilt, it is like burning regular gasoline in a car designed for unleaded. There is no initial difference in performance. In fact, the first fill-up is cheaper. But eventually the system begins to clog. Power diminishes; the wheels stop rolling.

Our churches are strewn with many such rusting hulks. After the stewardship campaign, the visitation blitz, and the Sunday school recruiting drive, inertia often sets in, the residue of being fueled with guilt.

What is missing is a creative environment where guilt-free, confident Christians pursue a few things wholeheartedly. Reaching this enriching environment does not require groping in dark, shrouded mystery. It has a lot to do with applying genuine biblical motivation.

The Christian walk is meant to take place amid freedom, peace, perseverance, and joy. Guilt is the warning signal that repentance (not more activity), forgiveness (not greater responsibilities), and restoration (not fancier incentives) are needed. Renewed freedom—release—is the result, not increasing bondage.

True *want-to* motivation instilled by God can be a reality. And it lasts.

Capturing and maintaining this lifelong motivation for God's work is no small sideline. It cannot be conjured up by intermittent trickery whenever attendance begins to lag or teaching vacancies appear. Rather, motivation is the consistent craftsmanship of a leader, and it demands continual nurture.

The Right Rewards

It is probably safe to say that the average lifelong member of a church has been "incentived" to death. Countless attendance thermometers have risen to the top as he invited friends to Sunday school rallies. Pins, Bibles, trips, titles, and strokes have been dangled, and he has pulled like the lead husky. But if the pressure is released or the campaign is less slick, does the performance continue? Has he learned a spiritual discipline, or has he simply salivated under the right stimuli?

A brief glance at God's original design, I feel, helps bring clarity and balance to our use of rewards.

In Genesis, people were created with something to do. From the very beginning, we were given the capacity to "rule over the fish of the sea and the birds of the air," to subdue the earth and fill it, and to work the garden. The *Imago Dei* is expressed in dominion and work.

This affects our view of motivation and reward. Work really matters! Our strivings do not have to relate exclusively to the sweet by-and-by. To stay motivated is to find reward in one's work. The Bible does not argue this; it assumes it. People are rewarded naturally by seeing that they are actually working, not merely staying busy.

The greatest reward is seeing progress and achievement in something you perceive as eternally significant.

But note: The newer the venture, the less developed my talents, the more fear I have. In these areas an achievable goal is paramount. When people are just beginning, immediate reinforcement is more important. If the job appears too big or the reward too far off, many will not risk the venture.

During the poverty days of seminary, necessity spurred my wife and me to begin building our own furniture. A close friend would often stop and chat, asking questions about lumber, costs, glue, and tools. When I challenged him to build some items for himself, he would back away, claim lack of aptitude, and retreat to his studies.

One Christmas, however, Phil wanted to surprise his wife with a small shelf for her spices. He came for advice, but what he got was encouragement. Every step was cause for counsel and deliberation. He drew plans, figured board footage, and asked about finish and mounting. Pointers may have been helpful, but the real task was helping to overcome the intimidation of actually doing it. Support was the real curriculum.

My friend has long since surpassed my ambitions and abilities. He has produced a houseful of early-American furniture, a custom-made wood stove, and, most recently, he designed and built an active solar family room! Small incentives don't guarantee great advances, but they help insure that first steps will be taken. And who knows where that will lead?

Though we discouraged people from asking, "What's in it for me?" we do well, whenever we begin a new program, to ask, "Can my people find legitimate and immediate reward in participating?"

Obviously, this can be abused. But remember, we are addressing only the initial steps of behavior, not the full scope of character development. It is possible to modify behavior without touching the person, so caution must be taken.

While raising our children, I discovered the power of rewards, as are a host of parents today facing the momentous task of potty training, room cleaning, or household chores. They are finding that good behavior can be launched by the promise of a shiny star on a chart. Similarly, the mountain of Christian discipleship can be broken down into achievable bits, culminating in appropriate rewards. Verbal kudos, personal affirmation, progress reports, and shared enthusiasm over a job well done are some of the tools to be employed. Paul did this with Timothy, Jesus with his disciples.

The impetus of incentive is most necessary at the beginning, and it can produce phenomenal short-term results. The key is the perceived value of the incentive.

On the bicycle trips we have taken each year with our youth group, we have traveled about 350 miles through the Colorado Rockies in five rather stressful days. One of the disciplines we want to instill during all those hours in the saddle is memorizing a life-related Bible verse each day. We have discovered an incentive that has never failed: No verse, no lunch. Verses get memorized!

On a one-week trip this produces tremendous results. As a weekly expectation in a Sunday school class, it would undoubtedly become a motivation problem. But the very experience of progress instills confidence and circumvents excuses. All of us need to be shown that we can succeed in spiritual enterprise. Sound incentives can insure a successful launch.

Worthy pursuits, noble achievements, and world-changing strategies all have discernible milestones. Incentive, extrinsic reward, and reinforcement need not be disdained if we understand their function. They are simply not the whole picture. Another aspect needs equal recognition.

Right Relationships

Without a shared excitement, any discipline can become lifeless plodding. Without a sense of teamwork and support, we risk burnout or latent bitterness.

Lone Ranger workers may continue for years, but they often have a degenerating perspective. They may feel unappreciated, perhaps perceiving themselves as martyrs. Frequently, this attitude is well disguised but flares up at the suggestion of change, improvement, or evaluation.

The Creation account provides us with a second essential quality of mankind. We are uniquely relational. Men and women were created to be in continuing relationships with God and each other.

In the Garden, Adam and Eve knew they mattered. This unconditional love from God and each other was to produce purpose, confidence, and lasting motivation.

This may help us understand why after seeing a midweek club ministry grow from twelve to one hundred, Mike and Sue burned out. They felt unappreciated. Their ministry, though productive, was isolated from pastoral or parental relationships. They labored on without appreciation, support, or integration with the whole. Their once-tenacious spirit gave way to disappointment, discouragement, and feelings of alienation. They had accomplished much, but how did it fit? Who cared? Did it really matter to anyone? Their hearts' questions went sadly unanswered. They needed a significant relationship to remind them it mattered to the people of the church, and most of all, to God. Their piece of the puzzle had eternal significance.

This dual aspect of man's nature helps us understand why we do not live by incentive alone. To simply move from one achievement to another without intimate personal partnership with God is meaningless. The greatest achiever of all time, Solomon, concluded that.

The mysterious internal combustion called motivation is sustained even in the absence of extrinsic rewards when one knows he or she is important to a worthy cause. This fuels tenacity—pushing ahead over obstacles, around barriers, and through darkness. When discernible reinforcements have long since disappeared, this motivation remains. It is sustained most often by sharing the enterprise in a quality relationship.

Crises poignantly remind us of our fundamental need for relationships. Conflict, grief, perceived failure, or loss of direction can quickly strip us of the virile motivation we knew during easier days.

Like every other person on planet Earth, conflict is my least favorite exercise. But as every Christian worker has discovered, it is sometimes unavoidable.

As I recently faced a season of misunderstanding and sleep-disturbing conflict, my motivation was sorely tested. Everything lost its luster; it was a time of emotional dullness, physical fatigue, and futile efforts. The phone became the conveyor of bad news; church growth seemed less important than personal survival.

In God's grace, however, I was surrounded with veteran spiritual warriors who refused to accept my interpretation of life. They painted the horizon a different color than I was able to see. While affirming my growing awareness of my blind spots, they doggedly refused to let me retreat. I was reminded of our corporate responsibility before God. My strengths were called upon, and my contributions were in demand.

Sustained by the richness of those relationships, the motivation to endure, learn, and overcome was kept alive. Motivation that lasts is fueled with love, respect, and appreciation. Much spiritual work, by its very nature, precludes external incentives. How precious at those times is the cadre of caregivers.

Right Purpose

Five couples met to discuss their Sunday school class. These were the faithful and the teachable. But their enthusiasm for their young-marrieds class was faltering. Week after week they experienced frustration. The atmosphere was not friendly, the lessons were not stimulating, and the social hours were sparsely attended. They weren't ready to quit—they were in it to the bitter end—but they were being reduced to mere endurance with little vibrancy or expectation.

As we talked, numerous agendas became apparent. Some felt the hour on Sunday needed more "meat." Others thought it should concentrate on relationships. Still others perceived too much time was wasted on coffee and donuts.

Once these struggles were heard, we reviewed our philosophy of ministry for adult Sunday school and placed its purpose in perspective with other ministries of the church. For us, Sunday school falls between the two extremes of Bible college and coffee klatch. We want to present life-size segments of sound biblical teaching wrapped in an outgoing, affirming atmosphere that anyone can enter. The standards for leadership need to be high, the entry qualifications low. We want to teach for the insiders but structure socially for the outsiders so they will be drawn in.

That automatically eliminated many of the frustrations. The couples saw it was not a choice of either/or, but both/and. They stopped fighting the agenda war and began planning for growth.

We brainstormed how the hour could be structured, leadership selected, and plans laid. That renewed the drive of those involved to make the class count. They were reminded of its relationship to the whole and were thereby liberated to concentrate on doing a few things well. Motivation returned.

A sense of duty isn't enough for a long-haul motivation; a sense of purpose is.

William James said, "Habit is the flywheel of society." Habits carry us through lives that are constantly under change and stress. Good habits in the church—such as giving, serving, teaching, or ushering—often thrive in people who have no elaborate or discernible reward system. Apparently they find meaning and joy in the enterprise itself. Such behaviors are the bedrock of church programs. We all value this kind of consistency.

However, purpose must be evaluated even among our most faithful people. The repetition of behavior without purpose can sour even the most faithful. Scripture repeatedly warns us of the dangers of performance without purpose, sacrifice without love. It is the essence of pharisaism. Giving is to be cheerful—work "as unto the Lord," service "in love," and correction "in gentleness." Workers can easily lose their connection to the whole enterprise, which not only stalls personal motivation but bottles up others who want to participate.

The more established the behavior, the more important its constant realignment to God's purpose. Means too easily become ends, thereby stifling freshness, growth, and teachability. Constantly renewing our vision helps us avoid complacency and averts demotivating battles over the status quo.

How can we help people maintain contact with ultimate purpose?

First, help people work together on tasks, rather than alone. Teamwork can be a guardian of perspective. Since people work is by nature an exercise in incompletion, we need others to help us maintain healthy vision.

Rick, Dave, and John have been working together in a singles ministry. As they have merged their separate gifts, strength has been obvious. There are still disappointments and an adequate dose of conflicts, but what is different in this shared stewardship is the endurance of vision. One lifts up the other (Eccl.

4:10). Teamwork places a net under wounded leaders. It catches them, nurtures, reminds, and recycles. Without that kind of support, spiritual warfare is often overwhelming. Rick, Dave, and John pray together, learn together, and struggle together. And together they have not lost sight of their ultimate purpose.

Second, I try to teach and preach how God's timeless plan is translated into human action. Even while propounding the Great Commission, it helps to give illustrations from living models. Not only does it illustrate the biblical command but also refuels the joyful purpose in our ministries. As Henri Nouwen has reflected: "If there is anything that makes the ministry look grim and dull, it is this dark, insidious anger in the servants of Christ." By using our sermons to point people to positive examples of faithfulness, we help build a motivated congregation.

One of these living illustrations is a church member who is now in his eighties. Most of his life was spent as a missionary and pastor. Now, because cancer has kept him housebound, he participates in our fellowship via cassette tapes. He recently wrote me a note: "Thanks so much for the tapes. We enjoy them and play them Sunday mornings, a little earlier than your service, adjusted to our aches and pains and weaknesses. We put on the clothes we would probably be wearing if we were going to the service. We follow the bulletin and the Scriptures, and we are ordering a hymnbook so we can follow the hymns."

To call that "motivation" doesn't do justice to the depth of such a life. Here is commitment spurred on despite diminishing returns, a flame that will not be extinguished by hardships, a life fueled by the worship of God himself.

This is the type of character we envision when we are fueling those who are beginning the journey. Self-sustaining fellowship with God is its own reward.

26

The Preacher as Pitchman

*I have no respect for the kind of preaching
that confuses selling with persuasion,
sales pitches with preaching the Gospel.*

—Ben Patterson

A hair salon in Minneapolis ran an advertisement recently that pictured Albert Einstein with the caption: "A bad haircut can make anybody look dumb!"

The now-deceased genius has appeared in a number of ads this year. Usually, however, he is seen promoting such high-tech products as computers and software. Apparently some ad agencies consider Einstein a universally accepted symbol of intellectual brilliance and technical mastery, the kinds of things we consumers hope to get a piece of in the purchase. Their rationale is simple, almost self-evident: If they can connect in our minds what he stands for with what they want to sell us, we can be persuaded to buy their products.

Gospel Pitchmen?

Persuade. Isn't that what we Christian preachers hope to do to people in regard to the Gospel? It may sound crass, but in the final analysis aren't we all in the business of selling the greatest product—Jesus Christ? Several people have suggested this is indeed the case, with one of them boldly calling Jesus himself the "greatest salesman who ever lived!"

Well, is selling the same as persuasion? Let's come at this from another angle. When we prepare a sermon or an evangelistic address, what do we want to see happen? Do we want hearers to change their beliefs or their behavior? "A false dichotomy!" you protest. True, but nevertheless an important distinction. Of course we want—God wants—those who hear his Word to change both what they believe and what they do. We shouldn't prefer one to the other.

But they *are* different. In selling, you change a person's behavior without changing his beliefs. In persuasion, you change a person's beliefs and, therefore, behavior.

Note how a good salesperson operates. If she can convince me that what I already believe about the value of intellectual prowess and technical mastery can be furthered by buying a certain word processor, she will have succeeded. She has no interest in a dialogue with me about the validity of those convictions; she wants only to connect those convictions with her product. If she can do that, everyone is happy. She is happy with her sales commission, and I am happy because my beliefs have remained intact; I think I have just bought something to further those beliefs.

That is selling.

Friendly Persuaders

Persuasion is quite another matter. Preachers with integrity face the difficult challenge of persuading us to change our *beliefs* and, therefore, our behavior. That forces them to grapple with us over things we hold on to for dear life. They must seek entrance into those most sacred precincts of our lives where we have enthroned false gods. They have to violate our preconceived notions about what is good and evil, right and wrong, true and false.

They may do this gently or brutally; they may appeal to our intellect or emotions; they may hold before us our fear of death or brace us with our love for life; they may use logic, they may use poetry; they may list propositions, they may tell stories. They may use any and all of the tools of rhetoric and debate. But, however they do it, they must present us with the radical, clear-cut decision between all we are without Christ and all we will be in him. Otherwise, the Gospel will not be preached; only a product will be pitched for our consumption.

In short, Christian persuaders must preach more than the gospel of the forgiveness of sins; as Jesus told his disciples, they must preach the gospel of *repentance* and the forgiveness of sins (Luke 24:47). Repentance, by definition, calls us to change our beliefs, our minds, our ways of thinking.

Mixed Messages

I want no one reading this to think I have a low opinion of salespeople per se. Provided the product is worthy and the needs and beliefs appealed to are legitimate, it is a worthy task to persuade the public your product will meet their needs—and, I might add, a task requiring extraordinary intelligence and resourcefulness.

But I have no respect for the kind of preaching that confuses selling with persuasion, sales pitches with preaching the Gospel. This kind of preaching uncritically appropriates current social myths and values and links them with the Gospel, making it the means by which those myths and values are attained or confirmed. This is deadly! So-called believers who have been sold on Jesus continue to believe the things they did before. The only change is that Jesus has now become an embodiment, an exemplar, a symbol of those enduring beliefs.

Do we in the contemporary church have a problem here? We certainly do in what styles itself as Christian media. Why the prominence of entertainers, athletes, millionaires, and politicians as gospel spokespersons?

There may be legitimate reasons, but I can also think of a crass one: they play there because they also play in the world.

To the worldly, these kinds of people symbolize legitimacy and success. As long as they can be linked with the gospel in some way, the gospel connects with legitimacy and success—as defined by the world.

The message, whether implicit or explicit, is that nothing really must change if you are to follow Jesus. Oh yes, sexual morality must be cleaned up, but beyond that you needn't worry. You can continue as committed to money, power, security, and recognition A.D. as you were B.C. The inferred difference is that you will now be more successful in the world than you were before.

How about Christian preaching?

I am not in a good position to judge since I am the preacher I hear most of the time. But if preachers' books give any indication, I have reason to worry that the gospel has been combined with our culture's preoccupation with psychological well-being. It's Jesus and your depression, Jesus and your marriage, Jesus and your obesity, Jesus and your anorexia, Jesus and your mid-life crisis.

Forgive me if my eye is jaundiced. People's needs are real, and the Gospel is a whole Gospel for the whole person. But God help us if these current concerns have written the agenda for our preaching and, worse, made us salespersons instead of Christian persuaders.

Beyond Persuasion

It is hard to persuade people about anything, much less the most radical thing of all: repentance and faith in Christ alone as the hope for salvation. It is more than hard; it is impossible! Who can change the way a person thinks and believes? Who is equal to the task? In the flesh, no one. Only God holds such power.

That is my point. When we substitute salesmanship for persuasion, we belie our faith in the supernatural power of God to use mere preaching to change people.

Each Halloween the kids in my neighborhood come to my door outlandishly dressed as robots and dragons, ghouls and superheroes. I always find it a delight to look into the eye holes of a Frankenstein mask and discover the cherubic little boy at the end of the street or hear the voice of the five-year-old girl next door coming through the witch's mouth. The costumes are fun to look at, but what makes them delightful are the children you find behind them.

To use Luther's very pregnant image, we preachers are God's masks. He hides behind us to do his work, not because he wants to be hidden, but because otherwise his unfiltered glory would annihilate those who see it. God really doesn't ask much of us; he calls for no heroic efforts in the pulpit. He needs nothing to commend him, no elaborate philosophical or cultural apologia to be believed. Above all, God doesn't need to be sold. All he wants is a little crack to shine through.

People will often be amused, even shocked, at the masks he chooses to wear. But they will be thrilled finally to have met him.

27

Saving a Sinking Ship

When I pay respect to the successes of the past,
I gain goodwill and trust.

—Bob Moeller

I remember when we had to set up seats in all the side rooms on Sunday mornings," the old man said. "We sometimes took two, even three offerings for missions in the morning service. Ah, those were the days."

We looked around at the sanctuary, now only a third full. The side rooms were cordoned off by cracking vinyl dividers. The room had the smell of emptiness.

So much had changed. In the last forty years, the city's social and economic composition had shifted. The young fathers and mothers of the glory years were now older and tired. Their grown children had moved to the suburbs.

"Jim, this church can have a significant ministry again," I said. "But we're going to have to adapt to the neighborhood we now live in."

His eyes revealed fear. Would "adapting" mean getting rid of everything familiar and precious to him? Would there still be a place for him and his wife and the pioneers who had founded the church?

Though my current church is healthy, over the years I've learned to identify the different groups left in a declining congregation. Each group has its own character, cause, and reasons for staying with a ship that is taking on water. To stop the decline, a pastor must have a working knowledge of each group and a strategy to motivate each one.

Pioneers

Unless a church is more than ninety years old, there are usually individuals who remember when the church began.

"Yes sirree, Pastor," said Stuart, a man in his late seventies. "I remember back in the '50s, coming here after work and digging out this basement by hand. It took all summer, but the pastor and several of us did it all ourselves."

As I looked at the large building, now located in a deteriorating inner-city neighborhood, I realized what a feat that must have been. Each shovelful of dirt had been carted out in wheelbarrows. Stuart had mixed his sweat with the mortar of this structure. Now his once-proud building stood aged and weather-worn. The paint was peeling. The cement stoop had pieces of concrete missing. The congregation was a quarter of the size it was when Stuart was young.

But Stuart was still there. Like most pioneers, he wasn't about to give up his homestead. He still talked about the twenty-four-hour prayer vigil the church held the day the first mortgage payment was due. He recalled the first Sunday that a couple from the congregation volunteered for overseas missionary service. All his children had been raised in the church.

Because of his seniority, Stuart served as unelected spokesman for the pioneers. When important issues came to a vote, the remaining pioneers turned in the pews to take their cue from him.

Pioneers are the last people to leave a declining church. They also suffer most when the dawn of ministry gives way to the twilight of dwindling attendance. Like the elders of ancient Israel, they weep when they remember the glory of the first temple.

What motivates pioneers to stay in a declining church? Like

E. Stanley Jones, the great missionary to India earlier this century, pioneers wish to bury their heart in the place they have served so long. That's why people in their nineties will ride city buses in twenty-below-zero weather to attend church. That's why they will show up for an evening program when everyone else is on vacation. That's why they will give to every offering, regardless of their fixed income. If there are ten people left in the church, seven will likely be pioneers.   .

It's tempting for pioneers to blame the younger generation for the losses and changes. After all, when the pioneers were young, the church prospered. There was rarely a shortage of volunteers or new members. There's often the suggestion that subsequent generations have dropped the ball.

"These younger people just aren't committed the way we were," I've heard pioneers say. "We brought our children to prayer meeting on Wednesday nights. Now they stay home and watch television."

Younger generations may accept the notion they're to blame. Stories of the spiritual triumphs of an earlier generation rub salt in younger members' wounds of guilt and inadequacy. The result may be mutual suspicion between the older and younger groups.

For the church to move forward, the blaming needs to be addressed. Everyone must realize the decline is due more to the changes in the community than the spiritual inadequacy of any one group.

Most pioneers are realistic; they know the glory days can never be recaptured. They will usually admit things have to change in order for the church to grow. What they're listening for is the assurance that their heritage will not be forgotten or trampled on. Pioneers' deepest need is for someone to understand and appreciate what they have accomplished.

When I suggested a seeker-sensitive Sunday afternoon outreach, I reminded the pioneers that they held similar services in the 1930s. Then, they had tried to attract children whose parents attended more traditional churches in the morning. They hadn't called their effort "seeker-sensitive evangelism," but that's what it was. The pioneers couldn't argue with the idea, and they appreciated the fact that I recognized and respected their past innovation and success.

It's better to stand on the shoulders than on the toes of previous pastors. When I pay respect to the successes of the past, I lose nothing. I gain goodwill and trust—two elements crucial to making changes that get the church growing. Then I can tap into pioneers' strong sense of commitment. When I suggested a barbecue on the front lawn to meet community neighbors, Stuart showed up in a pair of Levi's, ready to serve.

Curators

Another group that hangs on despite the growing shadows of sunset is the curators. Usually a much smaller group of people, it is most often made up of grown children of the pioneers. Their goal is to keep the church building open at all costs as a living memorial to their parents. Like curators in a museum, they wish to preserve the history and legacy of a previous generation.

Any change in program or worship is seen as an affront to the church's founders. It's as unthinkable as selling the furniture from a deceased parent's home. The church becomes a shrine not to be disturbed or altered. The curators' goal is not renewal but preservation. Even as the church loses ground, they desperately fight to keep things as they were.

There are two reasons why the curators are usually few in number.

First, most grown children of the pioneers moved away as young adults (often to more prosperous settings) and have little more than a nostalgic interest in the church's welfare.

Second, healthy Christians usually recognize that churches grow and change with the times. They find other ways to pay homage to their parents and grandparents than by keeping the same hymnbook in the pew for forty years.

Curators are crucial individuals in the church's makeup. Because of their staunch commitment to keeping the church going, they often assume significant roles. Many declining churches show a noticeable absence of adults between ages forty and fifty-five; the few that stay are often curators.

To motivate the curators toward growth and change is no easy task. In fact, they are usually more resistant than the pioneers. When I suggested a significant change in outreach strategy at a former church, it was a curator who dug in her heels: "What we need to do is get it back to the way it used to be."

The place to begin motivating curators is to assure them you share their deep desire to see the church doors stay open. You must convince them that the best chance of survival is to make certain adjustments. One effective means of getting curators on board is to dedicate a project to a person they have held in high esteem. Ultimately, you have to help curators see that a revitalized church, built on the historical and unchanging truths they hold to, is the most fitting memorial they can erect to their parents.

Dysfunctionals

In every declining church are people attracted by the confusion and chaos of long-term disintegration. These people are comfortable in a church of constant turnover and crisis; it may mirror the home in which they grew up. Instability and tumult are all they've known, so a church on the skids, scrambling to raise finances and always a month from disaster, makes them feel at home.

Dysfunctional people typically try to ingratiate themselves with the new pastor. Later, sensing a real or imaginary rebuff, they become hostile. "You're just the person for this place," they initially croon. Six months later, they question his spirituality. The pastor is first a messiah, then a false prophet.

In a previous church we served, a couple attempted to schedule virtually all of our free time to be with them. When we were unable to meet such unrealistic obligations, they turned on us and worked hard to turn others against us.

One characteristic of this group is that they fear newcomers and growth. One man said to me in tears, "Why do we have to reach out to new people? What's wrong with us? I'm a nobody out in the world. You bring in new people, I'll be a nobody again." He needed a great deal of assurance that he would still receive love and acceptance even if the church began attracting outsiders.

Motivating dysfunctional individuals to contribute to renewal requires generous amounts of strength and grace. You must both establish boundaries and return love for insults.

At one of our first churches, one family refused to speak to us for some time because of an offense we had supposedly committed. They were hoping we'd notice their manipulative behavior and ask what was wrong. But we decided to treat them as if we were still friends. We went out of our way to greet them and return smiles for scowls. It became increasingly awkward for them to ignore us. Eventually, they started speaking to us again.

One word of caution. It's important to discourage dysfunctionals from assuming high-stress leadership positions. All sorts of crazy behavior can kick in when the pressure is on. Steer such individuals toward lower profile, less stressful roles.

In the end, as you model healthy relationships and responses to life, these individuals may discover there is a better way to cope with life. As they sense love and affirmation within clear boundaries, they can learn to make significant contributions to the renewal of the church.

Stand-by Passengers

Another group you'll often find in a failing church are those who have packed their bags and decided they're on the next lifeboat out if things don't improve soon.

Stand-by passengers are typically gifted, upwardly mobile

individuals who are frustrated and exhausted by the problems at the church. They often have children at home and are worried about the lack of organization and quality programs for their kids. They have often lost close friends to other congregations. They feel socially isolated and under pressure to make a change themselves. All they want is a church that works.

You have only a short window of opportunity to persuade the stand-by passengers to stay. If you can't produce signs of recovery and growth soon, they're gone.

What stand-by passengers need most is hope, some sign that things aren't going from bad to worse. They need to know you believe things are going to change.

When I served as an interim pastor years ago, I demonstrated my faith in the church's future by bringing my family to all the services. We tried to communicate that we believed in the church and that we were there, body, soul, and spirit.

You will lose a number of stand-by passengers. Rarely can you make things happen fast enough to persuade certain people to stay. These people often become outside donors, assuaging their guilt for leaving by mailing a check once a month.

Even so, I have also watched families tear up their tickets and choose to stay. A few well-attended events may be enough to persuade stand-by passengers to unpack their bags.

In one struggling church, we held a successful film festival. The room was packed, something people hadn't seen in a long time. One stand-by came up to me smiling and said, "I didn't know the floor could hold this many people." He stayed to take a volunteer position in the church.

The Remnant

In every church that has suffered a slow, painful demise, some remain because they are convinced God will revive their church. They belong to what the Old Testament writers referred to as "the remnant in the land."

These saints faithfully teach a Sunday school class with only three children in attendance. They serve on boards and help plan church conferences they know will be poorly attended. They drive aging vans to pick up children and are always the first to volunteer for a new outreach program.

At first blush, these people seem out of touch with reality. Can't they see the church is nearly empty? That the choir has only eight people in it? That the parking lot is growing weeds?

The answer is yes. They know the church has no money, the pews are empty, and the basement smells of mold. But they don't walk by sight, they walk by faith. They have a quiet conviction that the church will once again serve the purpose God intends for it. Like Abraham and Sarah, they continue to believe the impossible.

It's not difficult to motivate this group. They pray, they serve, and they rarely complain.

When a giant food company donated 14,000 sealed hot dogs (with a shelf life of ten years) to our church, one of the remnant went home and began experimenting with recipes. He took all the canned goods available in our food pantry and devised meals that tasted delicious. He then passed out recipe cards to the needy who came for the food. That's the stuff the remnant is made of.

Motivating the remnant involves acknowledging their faith and believing with them that better days will return for the church. Though I was their pastor, I learned more from the remnant about trusting God than I ever taught them.

Allies United

One fascinating story from D-Day involved the 101st Airborne Division. Shortly after midnight on June 6, 1944, elements of the 101st parachuted into the darkness of France. Their mission was to link up with one another, then secure the key bridges and crossroads for the soldiers who would land on the beaches later that morning.

As often happens in war, things didn't go as planned. Heavy

cloud cover and poor visibility forced planes to scatter before they reached their drop zones. As a result, soldiers were dropped miles from one another all over the French countryside.

In the early morning darkness and confusion, General Maxwell Taylor, commander of the 101st Airborne, found himself all alone in the pitch black. When he spotted another soldier groping his way through the darkness, he demanded the individual identify himself. It was one of his troops, as lost and frightened as he.

The two were so overjoyed to find one of their own that they put aside military protocol and hugged each other. "It was at that very moment I knew we were going to win the war," said General Taylor.

When various groups in a declining church, separated and isolated by discouragement, link up again in a common cause, the tide of events will change. As history demonstrates, allies joined together in a common cause can win great victories.

28

Developing an Eager Church

An equipping ministry demands a change of attitude in both full-time staff people and the church as a whole.

—George Mallone

S andy called me with a simple request: "George, a friend of mine is in the hospital. Would you go and share some comforting words?"

I'm all for hospital visitation and helping a friend, but at that moment my ministerial priorities outweighed my ministerial guilt. Mustering up my courage and attempting to be as empathetic as possible, I said, "Sandy, my job is to equip you to do the ministry, not to do all the ministry myself. It is your job to visit your friend. There are three ground rules for hospital visitation: don't sit on the bed, don't stay too long, and pray and read the Word with your friend before you leave. When you have done these things, call me back, and I'll share some more tips."

You can imagine how I felt when the conversation ended. All afternoon I wondered if I had done the right thing. *Am I being lazy? What am I getting paid for? Am I a pastor or not? Don't pastors march hospital hallways every visiting hour?*

But after a few hours, new thoughts began: *I'm committed to the full employment of every believer. Putting that into practice may create a few awkward moments in relationships with people, but if I love them, teach them, and have confidence in their ministry, someday they will be off the spiritual welfare rolls and be full, active partners in ministry.*

Benjamin Franklin once commented that we were better off not knowing two things: how sausages and decisions are made.

Another thing we are better off not knowing: the number of pastors who proclaim the priesthood of all believers but in practice function by *sola pastora* ("pastor alone").

Given our usual seminary experience, this is not entirely unexpected. Much of our formal theological training has left us unprepared. In homiletics we learned to preach. In Christian education we learned to teach. But where were we taught how to train?

At our church we have decided to make an effort to train others. In many ways we're still learning, but we're making progress. Here are four steps we've found that enable pastors and churches to equip people to assume ministry.

Attitude Adjustment

An equipping ministry demands a change of attitude in both full-time staff people and the church as a whole.

Redefine the role

Over time, begin to redefine your role as one who equips others for ministry rather than one who does all the ministry. Describe yourself as a pastor among fellow pastors rather than as the pastor of the church. You will need to say these things from the pulpit so people begin to hear and see you in a different light. At the same time, you must affirm them, encourage them in their gifts, and although they may not have your training, show them they are necessary and useful for building up the body of Christ.

Design structures that fulfill these goals

It does no good to advocate giftedness and not provide structure for it to work. Church structures, therefore, must be designed to help *all* believers minister. Here's one example.

I am the primary teacher in our church. But I believe there are more teachers and preachers in the community, and they deserve the privilege of growing in their giftedness. One way to encourage this growth is to preach no more than 65 percent of the sermons. The remaining Sundays are not given to travel or speaking in other places, but to hearing those in our community who are growing in their preaching gifts. It demands that I listen to their teaching, record my response, and spend time with each speaker, providing affirmation and giving suggestions for improvement. It also means keeping them up-to-date on study materials and teaching resources, and giving them further opportunities to preach.

Know your God-ordained priorities

Priorities in ministry are seldom a choice between good and bad, but are frequently between good and better. It would have been good for me to visit the woman in the hospital; it was better to equip Sandy to do it. And if time permitted, the best would be to go with Sandy to visit the woman and to provide her with guidance as she continued to visit.

The important thing is that our God-ordained priorities are clear in our minds so we can handle the myriad requests. When a request to minister comes, I ask myself three questions:

- Can someone do this better than I?
- Is this an equipping opportunity?
- Does this fit in with my goals and objectives?

At times, various pastoral needs will overrule these questions, but where at all possible, ministry should be given over to our fellow priests.

Delegate in faith

If people are to grow in their gifts, we must be prepared to give ministry to them. By faith, we must believe that God can use them as well as ourselves. God's plan will not be thwarted because we can't be there. The more time we spend equipping others, the more confidence we will have that they can do the job.

Work yourself out of a job

We demand this of our overseas missionaries but allow ourselves to be exempt. Genuine church growth is not merely bigger churches, but more churches with a higher percentage of ministry participation. Consequently, we should be reproducing people who can plant new churches. This may mean that you equip a team and then leave to start a new work.

Working yourself out of a job, however, is fraught with identity struggle. More than one equipper has questioned, "How can I grow in my gifts if I am constantly giving ministry away? Will there be a place for me at the end?" Both are legitimate concerns; I have felt them deeply. But I can assure you that equippers will never run out of work to do or a place to belong. As to the identity crisis, it will be real. It will also be the fertile soil for learning the nature of servanthood. Ultimately, it doesn't threaten identity; it provides it.

Prepare for flak

An energetic equipping ministry leaves little time for lingering at high tea. You may not be at every social event or committee meeting. An educated congregation, still having the traditional role in mind, will no doubt have some questions about your absence. Graciously answer those concerns, but stick to your equipping priorities. You are a servant of Christ, called to do his bidding. You are not a slave to people's notions of your calling.

Gift Exposure

Eleven years ago I could not carry a tune in a bucket (I still sing pretty poorly). At the same time, I was exposed to men and women who had gifts in leading worship and I began to covet those gifts for our church. I remember watching one pastor lead his congregation in singing for forty-five minutes. There was no musical accompaniment, only his gentle voice leading them. I saw then that music was not only a performance gift but a gift for gathering the body together in collective worship. I went home and began (somewhat nervously) to model this in our own community. From this beginning, I took every opportunity to expose myself to as many worship leaders as I could find.

Giftedness needs exposure

As those called to equip others, we need as much exposure as possible to all the gifts. You may not have a particular gift personally (prayer for healing, for example), but you need to know what the gifts are and who can train your community in a given ministry. For me, this has meant traveling on my sabbaticals, attending one or two conferences per year, and making sure I am acquainted with the other pastors in my area. The latter has led me to a fellowship of some forty men and women who meet every two weeks for prayer and worship. The spillover from this meeting is that we exchange equipping ministries with one another. I led a workshop on facilitating congregational worship in Bob's church, and he led a workshop on evangelism in mine.

As we have been trained, people in our congregations will be equipped through exposure to real-life situations. Here is an example: Graeme was an unpaid intern in our church. He contributed twenty hours a week to study and ministry. In return, I spent time with him in reading tutorials and lectures. One such lecture dealt with church discipline. It was pretty much the simple transfer of teacher's notes to student's notebook, except for a few personal illustrations I was able to give.

A short time later, as a co-leader in a small home group, Graeme was confronted by a problem demanding discipline. Our elders decided to let the house group handle the discipline and not involve themselves unless it was absolutely necessary. No doubt Graeme felt in over his head, but he had been trained in the principles of biblical discipline, and I was sure his exposure to this real-life situation would be beneficial. It was indeed, for Graeme successfully led the group through the process of discipline and ultimately saw the restoration of the person back to the church. The equipping opportunity had been married to life exposure and produced a mature disciple.

Ministry Laboratory

I shudder at the memory of my early years of preaching. Just looking at my notes from those days produces a sense of disbelief and shock. But my gracious congregation at that time believed the principle that gifts grow in an experimental climate. Giftedness does not emerge into maturity all at once but slowly develops through trial and error, affirmation and correction. The tolerance I was granted as a young preacher needs to be extended to all.

An equipping church will foster a climate of experimentation with all the gifts. One year we ran a "gifts fair" in the church for two successive evenings. Over thirty workshops were offered in which people had an opportunity to learn about some of the gifts available to believers, see these gifts in action, hear how leaders grow in their giftedness, be warned of some of the pitfalls, and be given suggestions for discovering and using one's gifts. These workshops included the areas of helps, administration, working with prisoners, worship leadership, drama and dance, photography, writing music, preaching, counseling, ministry with the handicapped, and leading evangelistic Bible studies. As limited as this was, the climate invited people to experiment and see where and how God wanted to use them.

One of the primary places for gift discovery and affirmation is in small-group meetings. Within a relational environment, people can share their spiritual desires for ministry. When someone wants to use a gift, there is a good chance God has put that desire there. Spiritual pride can occasionally skew this principle, but generally we should encourage people who volunteer a gift.

The small group should manifest an attitude of expectation. If Karen believes God has given her gifts in songwriting, then we want to bring this before the group in prayer and give Karen a chance to share her compositions. We know she is only a beginner and her self-image and confidence are shaky, but affirmation and careful evaluation will help her to take the next step. As the group gives Karen opportunity to minister and expects her to grow, she most likely will. The group may encourage her to share one of her songs in the Sunday service. Whether she does a great job or falls flat on her face, the group is there to encourage her in the process and to give helpful suggestions.

Decentralizing Strategy

Few of the things we have discussed so far will be possible if a church retains the old wineskins, so to speak. The pastoral team may have a new attitude about equipping ministry, but it will be defeated if there are no structural changes.

The average church today is highly centralized. Everything happens at the church building (the "successful" church is open seven nights a week), and the senior pastor or one of the paid staff usually administers the program. Performance by a few is the norm over against participation by many. Attendance and passivity are stressed at the expense of interaction and leadership. This being the case, a highly centralized church will need fewer equipped people for its ministry. Unfortunately, it will also sacrifice the priesthood and giftedness of the believer to see this happen. A decentralized philosophy, on the other hand, demands more equipping because everyone is working.

In our church, the decentralization strategy becomes visible on four levels: personal, small-group, congregational, and citywide. Each level builds on the previous one.

The basement: personal and family development

In any building, the foundation is most important. So it is with building a body of equipped saints. Individual growth and family strength is the foundation. Growth can't happen without individuals involved daily in Bible reading, meditation, and prayer. But seldom do we take these practices seriously enough to teach how they are done and provide the necessary materials to do them.

Our congregation writes its own study guide to lead members through personal study, discussions with spouse and children, and preparation for the next Sunday's worship.

First floor: interpersonal and small-group development

From the foundation, we build the ground floor—interpersonal relationships and small groups. Four sections make up this level.

First, personal discipleship—the design is to have everyone learning from an older, more mature Christian and then sharing information and life with a younger believer. Bible-reading programs, Scripture-memory covenants, and prayer partnerships all play a part. Each of these involves some training and equipping.

Second, hospitality. As Karen Main's book *Open Heart, Open Home* suggests, hospitality and entertainment are two different things. It is essential that we train in the ways of hospitality. We've had special workshops to discuss the dilemmas of hospitality and how to get out of the entertainment rut.

Third, friendship evangelism. Most people come to Christ through contact with Christian friends or family members. Our emphasis should be upon sustaining contact with non-Christian friends and slowly winning the right, by our character and service, to share Christ with them. We try to train people in ways of friendship evangelism.

Fourth, household groups—probably the single greatest tool for gift discovery and development. Ranging from ten to twelve people and meeting in homes for up to three hours per week, these small units are able to know one another in an atmosphere of study, sharing, worship, prayer, and mission. House-group leaders in our fellowship are designated by the elders and serve as the primary pastoral team for their groups.

To keep our twenty-five house leaders encouraged and growing, we provide monthly training. Let me share one example.

As one who tours all the house groups to observe our leaders in action, I noticed that some were doing a poor job of leading Bible studies. That night I gathered five leaders in the center of the room and led an inductive study for them. The other twenty leaders sat on the sidelines with evaluation sheets to critique my leadership. Did I answer my own questions? Did I draw out the quiet and shy person? Were my application questions relevant to where people lived? At the end of the study, people shared their reviews. The leaders all agreed they could now lead a study more effectively because it had been modeled for them.

People are equipped when the activity is modeled and discussed at the same time. Demonstrate, analyze, and affirm.

Second floor: large groups and congregation as a whole

The traditional church sees the Sunday service as the performance of the few and the best, which is quite different from Paul's description found in 1 Corinthians 14:26. Although he believed in forms for worship (e.g., the Lord's Supper in 1 Corinthians 11), Paul also advocated a system in which believers were given freedom to share in that service. Such involvement can be greatly enhanced by equipping more people to participate on a regular basis.

Let me highlight that *major change* in the church does not happen at the Sunday-service level, no matter how good your preaching. Radical change begins at the foundational level and moves up to the congregational level. Sunday services are only an expression of vitality experienced at the personal, family, interpersonal, and small-group levels.

In addition to Sunday services, we also use large-group activities to train people. Saturday seminars, weekly training programs, weekend retreats, summer camps—all are excellent tools for developing effective workers for the mission of the church.

We encourage large groups to become involved in *extensive* evangelism. While friendship evangelism (*intensive*) focuses on friends and relatives, extensive evangelism reaches beyond the borders of our friendships to people unknown to us. Consequently, activities such as door-to-door visitation, open-air preaching, and evangelistic dinner parties can be great opportunities to train people to share their faith.

Third floor: citywide ministry

Every congregation needs opportunities to participate with other believers in a city for the purpose of proclaiming Christ and demonstrating the unity of the church. Crusade evangelism, inter-church worship rallies, and corporate demonstrations for social justice are a few examples. Each opportunity carries the potential for equipping.

These four levels we have looked at offer dozens of opportunities for people to be trained and to employ their gifts. Again, this is not a program but a strategy for decentralizing the church so that more people fulfill their God-given ministry.

"Outrageous—the whole process is outrageous," you may be saying. "It would never work in my church. We can't even recruit enough volunteers to serve on our committees!"

Maybe that's the point. Maybe believers are tired of fitting into fixed slots that have no relationship to their giftedness. Don't you feel this anxiety from time to time? An equipping model of the pastor-teacher is one starting point in the emancipation of God's entire priesthood.

29

Romancing the Congregation

Instead of mechanical procedures, my approach to leadership better resembles a courtly romance.

—Joel C. Hunter

I n seminary I thought of the local church as a complex engine needing a mechanic. And that mechanic was me. My best move so far in ministry has been to toss that image away.

The local church is not a machine. It is more like a person with a complex personality. Christ pictured this person as his bride. Certainly she has different aspects to her personality, but when I get bogged down trying to analyze them, I lose passion for our life together.

Instead of mechanical procedures, my approach to leadership better resembles a courtly romance. I nourish the same attitude toward my congregation as a suitor would toward his sweetheart. The results have been outstanding in church growth and development. Following are a few personal examples of this approach.

From Court to Courting

In my first board meetings, I assumed the role of defense attorney arguing for various progressive issues. I would lay out the facts about and advantages of air conditioning, for example. Prior to the meeting, I would make a guess as to who would be for air conditioning and who would be against it, carefully arranging my arguments with those categories of voters in mind. Or I might plead the cause for a new missions emphasis, quoting scriptural precedent, chapter and verse. The juries were always sympathetic, but several problems became painfully, consistently evident.

First, decisions were largely negative because of counterissues: "We don't have enough money right now" or "If we support one project, we have to support the other." Not much was said about the needs of individuals.

Second, my relationships with "jury members" were strained after a few meetings. Every comment seemed to bear a suspicious hidden agenda.

I once believed that church conflict paved the way to progress. All I needed to do was see that the right side won. Now I view conflict as a civil war within a person (the church), a war that gains no new ground. Progress can only be made as conflict is healed and forgotten. A house divided cannot hear the invitation of the Master: "Follow me." Now I work to deemphasize fragmentation and emphasize invitation to mutual adventure with Christ.

Many romances begin as business relationships and progress to personal intimacy. Unfortunately, too many lay/clergy relationships regress instead of progress. They begin with a desire for personal intimacy, but when the business aspect must be executed, the warmth is executed too. Some of us pastors have been attracted to heading a church ... whose *heart* we have never known. The most effective leaders know that when you inspire the heart, the rest follows.

Eventually I concluded that my approach to church business was ineffective, to say the least. I took a second look at Jesus' style. He had so much more going for him than facts and arguments. He was more winsome than winning; he exercised more influence than control. His approach was more intuitive than formulated, his authority more sensed than seen.

In matters of church business, I began to ask myself, "Why do I want this item passed?"

My conclusion: "Because we can do it together in love to be constructive for God." Then it dawned on me as it dawns on every suitor who is sweet on a girl: "It doesn't really matter what we do together as long as we *are* together."

The word "court" became a verb instead of a noun. Issues became secondary—more of an excuse for us to be together. Personal attention and respect in the middle of the business of the church was like manna in the wilderness. Eventually we became reluctant to make decisions that would interfere with the love and warmth necessary for progress. Courtship had replaced one-upmanship.

From *Pre*determined to Pre*determined*

After some months of dating, flirtation, and intrigue with my wife-to-be, the questions arose: *Is our relationship merely a product of chance?* or *Are we meant to be together by some higher plan?*

Tracing the unusual coincidences that led to our meeting, we decided it was the latter. In our more romantic moments we still cherish the fact that our marriage was "meant to be." It is the icing on the cake.

What most fascinates me, though, is that this conviction is even more valuable in our struggles. While the implications of predetermination provide fodder for theological debate, the effects of predetermination on us are remarkable. It adds a sense of permission, power, and stewardship to the relationship.

When I met each of my congregations, we likewise were convinced that God's plan for us was being fulfilled. Here, too, a sense of divine leading from the start (*pre*determination) energized and motivated me to carry out my part of the enterprise to the best of my ability. But the conviction also gave me a determined sense of accountability (pre*determination*) to accomplish the quest.

It had specific effects as well. In seminary, I considered Bible study and prayer to be matters of personal edification. In the church, these exercises provide my instructions from the Matchmaker. In seminary, my worth depended upon how much I knew. In a church relationship, my power comes from how consistently I love.

Not too many years ago I found myself facing a very angry parishioner. As he told me how little he thought of my ministry, I grew quiet, trying to defuse the confrontation. Afterward, I was pretty shaken up and found myself with two conflicting thoughts. At first I raged, *Who needs this? I'm a good minister with solid gifts. Maybe I ought to get out of here and find a church where everyone will appreciate me!*

The irrational last half of my first thought sparked my second thought: *If God has placed me in this congregation, escape is not a valid choice. I suspect I—as well as my angry parishioner—can learn something by my staying.*

The idea that God has plans for *individual* lives is a great source of strength and cause for perseverance. Jesus expressed it when he said, "You did not choose me, but I chose you and appointed you to go and bear fruit—fruit that will last" (John 15:16).

People who believe they are a key part of the highest plan are people who have the key to behave on the highest plane.

From Screen to Screened

Our culture is now emerging from two decades in which people have pursued intimacy with reckless abandon. The hangover from this phenomenon still affects leadership styles.

The basic assumption goes something like this: "Leaders are people who need others to love them, but they can't be loved until they reveal themselves. The more they reveal, the more there is for others to love. So tell all!" While the basic theory is valid, many times the basic practice is not. The let-people-get-to-know-you-by-letting-them-go-through-your-garbage dynamic is neither appetizing nor particularly effective.

When I was fresh out of seminary, over a dozen years ago, I assumed the church was like the seminary community. I figured the congregation considered the pastor a colleague and peer. I was wrong. I did silly things. I remember telling an off-color joke in a men's group one day. I was trying to communicate my humanness. Maybe some did feel closer to me because I was not above them. I couldn't tell. What I could tell in the following months was that my ability to lead those men spiritually had plummeted.

Another time I responded to a parishioner's confession with, "Oh, don't be too hard on yourself. I've had those feelings, too, and never resolved them."

She shot back, "Then I've got to see someone else. I need help *up!*"

Projecting all I am and all I think for anyone to see on a huge screen is not bad. It's stupid. Let's move "screen" from a noun to a verb.

We need to screen what we reveal in the same way a wise suitor screens his conduct and conversation. Romance wants to weave a positive context for intimacy. Discretion is not deception. When we were dating, we first put our best foot forward. As the relationship grew to maturity, we gradually revealed weaknesses in proper perspective. Then "bearing one another's burdens" could be an act of intimacy rather than a form of exhibitionism. A congregation has the same initial needs as a girlfriend: They both need time to trust my best so I can trust them with the rest.

Before I share intimate information with people, I screen thoughts with these criteria:

- Am I revealing this for my benefit, for their benefit, or for the Lord's benefit?
- Can the people I am telling do anything about what I am revealing?

- Will their possession of this information increase my ability to help them?

I have decided not to bare my soul in wide-screen splendor without first screening the timing and content in light of the needs of the person of my affection.

From Grace to Grace

Question: What is the difference between attending a third-grade dance recital and watching Fred Astaire spin across the floor with Ginger Rogers?

Answer: Watching the one, you hope the dancers do well, but you'll applaud no matter what. Watching the other, you want to dance.

There are two aspects of grace, both positive. One involves our worth to our heavenly parent. The other involves movement, disciplined yet free, so impassioned it elicits our own self-expression. The first aspect of grace comforts, the second excites. In like manner, one aspect of romantic love is famously unconditional ("love is blind"). But the most powerful aspect of romantic love is that it exists to elicit reciprocal love.

Consider two preachers I've known. One preacher crafted his sermons in the most careful way. Each presentation was constructed correctly, performed with few mistakes, and rewarded with the appropriate, "That was a good one, Reverend." And surely God loved him in his efforts. Yet the sermons were mechanical, driven, brittle, and validated only by approval.

The other preacher's whole life gave his sermon integrity. He didn't present his sermon, his sermon presented him! The privilege of preaching consumed and fascinated him. He was spirited, confident, and flexible in the pulpit. He often changed tone and content in response to the expressions on people's faces. His sermons were valid regardless of any response, but there was definite response.

The difference between these two approaches is the difference between the Law and the Christ. One is an *export from self,* the other the *expression of self.* When the gift cannot be separated from the giver, it is an offering that creates a longing within the recipient.

Perhaps the most powerful element in both romance and ministry lies in the messenger's being so caught up in the message that the recipient is moved to respond. The highest evaluation of preaching—or any ministry of grace—is this: Do people move beyond accepting the unconditional love (grace) to offering themselves in response (graceful living)? The graceful pastor imparts both kinds of grace to the person (congregation) he romances.

Jesus tenderly turned power upside down. Instead of political power, he chose the kingdom of the heart, saying, "The kingdom of God is within you" (Luke 17:21). This dimension of leadership goes further than principles of excellent pastoral practice; it snuggles up to the person's heart.

Those who find this dimension of ministry discover magnetism. Romance is not confined to football captains and homecoming queens; romance can and should describe the love affair between a pastor and his congregation.

30

Up to the Challenge*

*The redeeming and rebuilding of human lives is
exceedingly more difficult than building widgets or
delivering predictable services.*

—Bill Hybels

A fter twenty-four years of leadership, I have come to believe
five truths about leadership in the church:

1. *I believe the church is the most leadership-intensive enterprise in society.*

My friend runs a company with about 3,000 employees. He
says he wants to relax after retirement and lead a church: "It
doesn't have to be a Willow Creek-sized church. Maybe just
7,000 or 8,000 with some growth potential." I told him that leading a church will ruin his retirement because the church demands a higher and more complex form of leadership than
business does.

I've been on both sides. Running a business is challenging,
but the leader of a company has a clearly defined playing field
and enormous leverage with his or her employees. The business leader delivers a product or service through paid staff who
either get it done or get replaced.

Church leadership is far more complex than that. The re-

* Adapted by permission from an address delivered at the 1995 Willow Creek Leadership Summit Conference.

deeming and rebuilding of human lives is exceedingly more difficult than building widgets or delivering predictable services. Here's why:

Every life requires a custom mold. You don't stop the line in a factory every time a product comes down it. In church work, we're developing individual, custom-made lives. We stop the line for every life.

I've read books about Napoleon, de Gaulle, Eisenhower, MacArthur, Patton—all the great military leaders. I don't want to minimize their capabilities or the courage it took to charge a hill in time of battle, but I've wondered, *What would it have been like for some of those leaders to have had to work it out with their deacons before they charged up the hill? How well would they have done if they had had to subject their plans to a vote involving the very people they were going to lead up the hill? How would the whole military system work if you took away the leadership leverage of the court-martial?*

Anyone could build a church with that kind of leverage! "Teach a Sunday school class or go to the brig." "You call that an offering? Give me fifty push-ups right now." *That's* leverage!

The church is utterly voluntary. In the final analysis, we have little or no leverage, no real power over anybody we lead. At Willow Creek we've had people attend our services week after week and then create trouble throughout the church and tap every resource we have. Then when they cross one too many lines and the elders bring correction or discipline, they bail out of the church or even sue.

To mobilize an utterly voluntary organization requires the highest kind of leadership.

The church is utterly altruistic. When leading a business, you can hire a bright, energetic young employee and say, "Here's our vision. Here's your part in it. Here's your salary, your perks, your car, your phone, your fax, your computer, your secretary, your office, your vacation plan. If you work hard, in five or eight years we'll make you a partner or invite you into the profit-sharing plan. Down the road, you'll probably make big money. There will be more perks, more time off. And when we sell this place in fifteen or twenty years, we'll all walk away transcendently wealthy. Are you interested?"

Who wouldn't be?

As church leaders, we tell prospective church members: "You're a depraved, degenerate sinner who's in trouble for all eternity unless you get squared away with Christ." (And that's the good news.)

Then we say, "We're going to ask you to commit five or six hours a week to service and two or three additional hours for training and discipleship. We're going to ask you to get into a small group where your character flaws will get exposed and chiseled at. We're going to ask you to come under the authority of the elders of the church and give a minimum of 10 percent of your income.

"Oh yeah, and you get no parking place, no reserved seats, no special privileges, no voting rights, no vacation, and no retirement program. You serve till you die. But trust us: God's going to make it worth your while in eternity."

In church work, people must be motivated internally. As the Scriptures tell us, unless the Lord builds the house, unless people have an internal "want to," leaders have no power, no leverage, no buttons to push.

When businesspeople in our churches give free advice—how we should be doing it—we need to say without malice, "It's not that easy, and it's not the same. It's apples and oranges."

2. *I believe there is a spiritual gift of leadership.*

Some people have it, some people don't.

In one of the spiritual gift lists, Romans 12:8, the apostle Paul essentially says, "If you have the spiritual gift of leadership, lead with it, and lead with all diligence." God alone decides who gets this gift and in what measure.

I've come up with a partial list of what spiritually gifted leaders do if they develop and use their leadership gifts.

They cast a God-honoring vision. Spiritually gifted leaders live in such a way that God invariably ignites within their hearts a compelling idea, a heartfelt yearning for some part of God's kingdom to advance. They start thinking about it, dreaming about it, and praying about it. Pretty soon, they start talking about it. They have lunch with someone and say, "Can you imagine what this part of the kingdom would be like if. . . ?"

Not long ago, I took the board of directors at Willow Creek to some inner-city ministries that we're funding and for which we are providing volunteer help. We were in an empty warehouse; it must have been ninety-five degrees. The humidity was incredible. But the person leading this ministry stood and said, "Imagine that corner of this warehouse filled with electrical supplies. A skilled worker from a church could stop here, pick up all the supplies he or she can use, and go to the home of someone in need and fix the wiring.

"Imagine pallets stacked high with drywall compound. When there are walls to be patched in the home of someone who can't afford to fix them, a volunteer could stop here and pick up the drywall and fix the holes.

"Imagine another pallet piled with blankets. In the winter, when the heat isn't working in someone's apartment, we could provide extra blankets."

I was reaching for my wallet! *That* is vision casting.

If you have the gift of leadership, God ignites in your heart a vision. You cannot *not* talk about it.

There is a tremendous amount of power released when a leader starts casting a godly vision. It draws people out of the woodwork. It gets bored spectators out onto the playing field.

They gather and align people for the achievement of the vision. Spiritually gifted leaders have the God-given capacity to attract, challenge, and persuade people. Then they assist them in finding their niche in the achievement of the vision.

Spiritually gifted leaders are almost shameless in the boldness with which they approach people. They can't understand why anyone wouldn't already be on board with them. People catch their enthusiasm.

Next, the leader says, "I'm going to find a role that fits who you are. You're going to grow and develop as an individual while all of us grow together in the achievement of the vision. This is a win/win deal."

Leaders do not use people. Leaders cast a vision until they find those who want to join with that vision. Then the leader commits to developing that person while together they achieve their dream. That kind of synergy and unity and teamwork is *powerful.*

They can motivate their co-workers. Motivation makes work fun. It can make thankless tasks exciting. It can make beaten-down people feel renewed and rejuvenated. People with the spiritual gift of leadership have a God-given ability to know what to say and how to inspire a variety of people.

I had an eighth-grade basketball coach who knew how to inspire me. I went to North Christian Grade School; on the other side of town was South Christian Grade School. We wanted to beat the stuffing out of those Christians on the other side of town.

I was just a little guy; my trunks came up to my armpits. In an important game, we were behind by a few points. As we players were walking back onto the court after a time-out, the coach encouraged us, "Okay, let's go get 'em."

But then he added, "Hybels, get back here." I came dutifully back.

"I think you're the only one with the guts to go out there and take that ball to the basket."

I thought my heart was going to explode. I knocked people over to get the ball to the rim.

That night they called me "His Airness." (Michael Jordan cashed in on the term, but it was first said about me that night!)

Gifted leaders have the ability to motivate and inspire.

They sense the need for positive change and then construc-tively bring it about. I do a lot of my summer study in a Burger

King restaurant in South Haven, Michigan. Right behind where
I sit is a side entrance door. It is a heavy steel door with a broken
hamper mechanism. Every time a customer comes in, the door
bangs shut loudly. It's metal on metal. The staff working the
counter look at each other every time as if to say, "Gee, that's
an aggravating sound. Why do people keep doing that?"

Then there's the problem of the temperature in the restaurant—it's always around sixty-two degrees. Way too cold for the
average human being. Customers walk up to the counter and
say, "Do you know it's freezing in here?" After they leave, the
people behind the counter say, "If they knew how hot it was
back here working over the stove, they wouldn't complain so
much."

I was reminded every day there was no leader in sight. A
good manager would say, "Fix that door! Set the air-conditioner
for the customer's comfort. If we need to add fans in the back
for employees, or if we need to rearrange some duct work or
something, let's do it. You don't freeze the customers out. They
pay our salaries."

Leaders have a nose for how to constructively bring about
change.

They establish core values. Leaders not only remind co-
laborers of their mission but also hold up certain standards and
values and lay out certain ground rules. A great leader says to
her team, "Okay, this is the hill we're trying to take. Here's the
role each of you is going to play. Along the way, this is how
we're going to communicate with one another; this is how we're
going to treat one another. And these are the values we're going
to hold up so that the process of taking the hill is a wonderful
experience for everyone."

They allocate resources effectively. A good leader is always
resource-conscious. A good leader asks, "What do we have in
the quiver? What tools, what funds, what talents, what techniques? How can we strategically invest these toward the fulfillment of the vision?"

Historically, the whole resource function of kingdom work

has been viewed with suspicion. Layworkers say, "Aw, let's not talk money." Leaders say, "Money is a big part of the whole and we can't ignore it."

They identify entropy. Leaders usually identify entropy in its earliest stages. A leader is vigilant twenty-four hours a day. He or she walks around and asks, "Where are the wheels starting to wobble? Where is this organization weakening? If we can identify it and find a solution *before* the wheels fall off, we can maintain momentum."

They create a leadership culture in their organization. This quality is absolutely counterintuitive. One would think that strong, gifted leaders would be concerned about emerging leaders maturing to the point of threatening their own leadership. Actually, the exact opposite is true of a spiritually gifted leader. The greatest thrill he or she can experience is the gradual achievement of the God-given vision through the combined efforts of developing young leaders who will someday carry the baton.

At Willow Creek, we host an annual leadership summit conference. I get choked up when I go from classroom to classroom watching Willow Creek leaders stand in front of groups of people and cast vision, inspire, and motivate about everything from programming to children's ministries. I go home on these nights thinking, *It doesn't get any better than this.*

This climate is at the heart of leading an organization. A leader creates a culture in which more and more people are at liberty to come forward and lead.

3. *I believe most churches unintentionally undermine the expression of the leadership gift.*

This doesn't necessarily mean there is anything sinister going on, but churches generally do this in at least two ways.

First, they undermine the expression of the leadership gift when they fail to teach about it. As a result, potential leaders among young men and women in the church think, *If my gift were valued in the church, it would be talked about as a valid gift*. They reason, then, that they might as well use it in the marketplace.

Why isn't the gift of leadership taught in the church? Most of the instruction that flows from our pulpits tends to come from people with teaching gifts, but few teachers understand what the leadership gift is and how it works.

Leaders don't usually "talk" about leadership because they aren't sitting around reflecting about it or analyzing it. And as a general rule, most leaders don't have a teaching gift, so they are not inclined to teach about it.

Second, churches undermine the leadership gift by implementing church governance systems that frustrate gifted leaders into oblivion. Leaders need a certain amount of room to operate, a degree of trust from the church or the organization in order to express their skill or gift. If you take away these opportunities, leaders will bail out, and no one can blame them.

I'm not suggesting we do away with boards and elders and deacons and by-laws. But within certain parameters, pastors and staff and layleaders with leadership gifts must be given real challenges to face, genuine hills to take, and problems to solve. Emerging leaders must be given enough room and enough trust from the church to be able to go out, spread their wings, and develop their gifts.

And yes, some mistakes will be made now and then. But overall the kingdom will make huge gains.

4. I believe almost everybody wants to be led.

In Matthew 9:36, Jesus weeps for the people in Jerusalem because they are wandering "like sheep without a shepherd." They are aimless. Without purpose. Jesus is speaking primarily of people's need for a savior and sovereign leader. But the imagery can also apply to a wider range of situations.

People without a leader are a people to be pitied. I feel sad when I see impoverished, exploited citizens in leaderless countries. I even feel for listless students in leaderless classrooms. It's not much fun to sit in a classroom where no goals are taught for the class and no one is going anywhere.

It's not much fun to be undervalued, underchallenged, underdeveloped, and undernurtured. If you've ever worked in a leaderless company, you have an idea what I'm talking about. How about a sports team without a leader? There is no hope of winning because there is no motivation.

On the contrary, have you ever played on a great team for a great coach? Have you ever worked for a growing company with a confident, challenging manager? What a difference.

I used to play on a park district touch football team led by Don Cousins, my associate pastor for seventeen years. We played against construction workers who gathered after work, semi-inebriated, with the sole purpose of hurting people. In one game, my job was to try to sack the quarterback; I was lined up across from a guy who was supposed to prevent me from doing that. I thought, *I'm going to run right over the top of him.* I was breathing hard, getting all pumped, when I looked up. The guy's eyes were bloodshot and he was drooling. I thought, *Maybe I'll just drop back in case the quarterback passes this time.*

We were smaller than most of our opponents, but we won almost every game we played. Don Cousins *led* that team. At the end of the season, if we had asked, "Anybody want to play next season under the leadership of Don Cousins?" every person in the league would have signed on.

One great writer about leadership says, "Most people are simply waiting for someone to call them out so they can rise above their petty preoccupations."

We can no longer afford to leave people without leaders in the arena of the church. May the church be the one place where people who come out of leaderless homes and schools and jobs and sports teams discover, maybe for the first time in their life, the excitement of being valued, being included, being told that they are indispensable for the achievement of a common vision.

5. *I believe the church is the hope of the world, and its renewal rests in the hands of its leaders.*

William Bennett, former secretary of education, said some time ago, "I submit to you that the real crisis of our time is spiritual. What afflicts us is a corruption of the heart and a turning away of the soul. Nothing has been more consequential in this societal demise than large segments of American society privately turning away from God. And to turn things around, there must come a widespread personal spiritual renewal."

I have to believe that's true. Who traffics in the spiritual transformation business? The church. I have come to see with crystal clarity that the church possesses the single ray of hope left in the darkening skies of human depravity.

The church has the life-transforming message of the love of Christ. The church has the instruction manual, the Bible, the guidebook for relationships and ethics and morality. The church has the gift of community to offer wayward and wandering and lonely people. The church can give people purpose by inviting them to become part of the transcendently powerful mission of world redemption.

But for the church to reach its redemptive, life-giving potential, it must be led and it must be led well. It must be powerfully envisioned, strategically focused, and internally aligned. Members must be motivated; the message preached. Problems need to be addressed; values established and enforced. Resources must be leveraged.

These things are the business of leaders. Which is why Paul said in Romans 12:8, "If [a man's gift] is leadership, let him govern diligently." Men and women, if you've been given the gift of leadership, for God's sake, lead. For the world's sake, lead. For the sake of lost people, lead.